WOMEN
WHO
DANCE *IN*
THE DARK

ALSO BY ATHENA LAZ

*Sisterhood of the Seers Oracle:
A 44-Card Deck and Guidebook**

*The Alchemy of Your Dreams: A Modern Guide to the
Ancient Art of Lucid Dreaming and Interpretation*

The Deliberate Dreamer's Journal

*Available from Hay House

Please visit:

Hay House UK: www.hayhouse.co.uk
Hay House USA: www.hayhouse.com®
Hay House Australia: www.hayhouse.com.au
Hay House India: www.hayhouse.co.in

WOMEN WHO DANCE IN THE DARK

AWAKEN YOUR INNER SEER
Through Myths, Dreams and Stories

ATHENA LAZ

HAY HOUSE
Carlsbad, California • New York City
London • Sydney • New Delhi

Published in the United Kingdom by:
Hay House UK Ltd, 1st Floor, Crawford Corner,
91–93 Baker Street, London W1U 6QQ
Tel: +44 (0)20 3927 7290; www.hayhouse.co.uk

Text © Athena Laz, 2025

Cover design: Barbara LeVan Fisher
Interior design: Karim J. Garcia
Interior figures: Athena Laz

The moral rights of the authors have been asserted.

All rights reserved. No part of this book may be reproduced by any mechanical, photographic or electronic process, or in the form of a phonographic recording; nor may it be stored in a retrieval system, transmitted or otherwise be copied for public or private use, other than for 'fair use' as brief quotations embodied in articles and reviews, without prior written permission of the publisher.

The information given in this book should not be treated as a substitute for professional medical advice; always consult a medical practitioner. Any use of information in this book is at the reader's discretion and risk. Neither the author nor the publisher can be held responsible for any loss, claim or damage arising out of the use, or misuse, of the suggestions made, the failure to take medical advice or for any material on third-party websites.

A catalogue record for this book is available from the British Library

Tradepaper ISBN: 978-1-83782-334-5
E-book ISBN: 978-1-4019-7955-3
Audiobook ISBN: 978-1-4019-7956-0

10 9 8 7 6 5 4 3 2 1

This product uses responsibly sourced papers, including recycled materials and materials from other controlled sources. For more information, see www.hayhouse.co.uk

The authorized representative in the EU for product safety and compliance is Penguin Random House Ireland, Morrison Chambers, 32 Nassau Street, Dublin D02 YH68, Ireland. https://eu-contact.penguin.ie

Printed and bound by CPI Group (UK) Ltd, Croydon CR0 4YY

For Sasha and Sophia

CONTENTS

Introduction: The Return of the Soul Voice ix

Chapter 1:   We Begin with a Medial Wolff 1
Chapter 2:   The Threshold of Entry 11
Chapter 3:   Mediatrix of All Graces 21
Chapter 4:   The Medial Woman's Mythic
             Journey of Initiation 35
Chapter 5:   An Ancient Language Is Evoked 43
Chapter 6:   The Baba Yaga Effect 61
Chapter 7:   Roll That Medial Ball Until You Land
             in the Wild Woods 87
Chapter 8:   When All Hope Is Lost and Returning Home 95
Chapter 9:   In the Silence, the Oracle Speaks 103
Chapter 10: Learning to See and Hear in a Sacred Manner 119
Chapter 11: Understanding Your Own Intuitive Abilities 139
Chapter 12: The Shadow Side of Being Medial 167
Chapter 13: The Modern Mediatrix and the
              Creative Principle Realized 181
Chapter 14: Tools for Wholeness 183
Chapter 15: The Wildflowers of Your Heart 197

Acknowledgments 203
About the Author 205
Endnotes 207

Welcome to the literary gateway that allows us to journey together.

You, where you are right now, and me, where I once was, writing in the cave of wonders so that both you and I may hear the Soul speak.

INTRODUCTION

THE RETURN *OF THE* SOUL VOICE

We are all Medials, and we are all born knowing.

Have you ever had that feeling that you just *knew* something was about to happen? Or experienced a time when your intuition spoke to you so clearly that you knew exactly what to do? Or perhaps you've had a dream that felt almost too real? In those special moments, you were in touch with something larger than linear cause and effect.

You were in touch with the Medial Woman herself.

Archetypally, the Medial Woman represents the intuitive, mediator, and mediumistic functions within the psyche. Sister seer to any Wild woman, she can appear as a mythic figure, a disembodied voice, or simply as a dream guide. She is the part of you that inherently knows where to go and what to do, the part of you that whispers helpful insights and deeper knowings, if you are open and willing enough to receive them. As a mediator of the limen, Medial Woman teaches us about our own multidimensional awareness. She beckons us toward an inward journey of initiation and awakening so that we can reclaim our wholeness. Yet we are often taught to ignore this helpful and medial aspect of ourselves. This is the great unlearning that we must all undergo and to which this book contributes.

This book is a written remembrance of this potent but often dismissed power that lies within us all—that lies within you.

Sometimes we act in order to not see,[1] and yet the modern era we live in requires us *to really look*—to see the greater truth of who we are, what we have created, and where we are headed. Our times call for a collective restoration of this intuitive and balanced knowing for heightened transformation and well-being. We are called to work with the Medial archetype within to mediate any severe divides within ourselves and out in the world. We must strengthen our ability to commune with the unseen worlds of Spirit as well as the deeper recesses of the psyche. The final result: a recognition of our ability to alchemize our own reality as well as that of the world around us.

Where the dirt meets the earth and where all things can be seen, that is where we will meet the Medial Woman within. Let us begin.

CHAPTER 1

WE BEGIN
WITH A
MEDIAL WOLFF

Like all good stories, we must start at the beginning. But how do we do that when we are touching a force that is so mysterious in nature? One that runs through time and space itself—touching multiple realities woven into the destinies of millions of lives? We look into history, and we see that the stories of our collective ancestry, heritages, and identities all come together into what we call "our life." We look at the individual within the collective, and we learn about the psyche and this mysterious Medial force that weaves itself through it all.

Let's begin by considering the feminine and the masculine. Here we see ancestors, mothers, daughters, and sisters—each with their unique stories located in specific historical realities. We *know* that the feminine has suffered severely throughout history—witch trials, slavery, forced marriages, being sold into prostitution—and that this suffering and oppression continue. And yet, for the sake of balance, the art of temperance, we must also look at how the counterpart has suffered: wars, slavery, persecution, the fierce nature of survival, and living through many historical realities where emotions, nurturance, and softness were forcibly removed from the conversation and way of life.

These are by no means absolute examples; they are simply guidelines into a larger picture and generalized experience that many people have lived through. The masculine and the feminine wounds often arise from different ancestral traumas or points of pain. And as a result, they often require different forms of healing. This system also doesn't reflect marginalized groups of people who aren't part of these categories yet have suffered greatly too. Pain is pain, and healing requires an in-depth look at the root of suffering no matter how we identify with it.

In haste, we often look for a solution, any solution, to offer a pathway out of this collective suffering, yet this is not the way. We must slow down and survey the collective heritage that *we as humans* come from. When we do that, we step out of the blame game, and we move into a higher perspective, **a perspective that can give us peace, clarity, and positive Spiritual direction for all.**

So, the beginning of this story requires a higher perspective from you, my reader. A perspective that requires that you look at the human experience like multiple facets of one shining diamond. Each facet is part of the whole: valuable and unique, with its own story shining as a light for others, reminding us that we are all in this together. **Our time calls for this very remembrance: We are all one in our humanity.**

Our archetypal teacher, our penultimate Medial Woman, arises into collective consciousness to awaken us to this remembrance. She has sent out a call which you have answered simply by reading these words. Her power is fierce and strong, yet her greatest strength is that her power is rooted in her compassion. You will come to learn over the course of these pages that you are equally fierce and strong and that it is up to you to consciously choose what to do with your power. Will you help to restore healing and balance in the world at large? Will you use your inner knowing for the good of everyone—including yourself?

Our capacity for healing, wholeness, and compassion is just one thought away, as our Medial Woman can dive into the depths of any suffering and arise from it like a phoenix renewed. By virtue of her support, so can you. Our regenerative powers are intrinsic. She shows us that the psyche is whole and complete, and that it can be restored to a place of well-being at any point.

The Medial Woman comes from the mind of the late analyst Toni Wolff. Toni wrote about the Medial Woman in a discourse called *Structural Forms of the Feminine Psyche*. She had the courage to write aspects of the Medial Woman into being during the 1950s, when women were often thought to be "hysterical" simply for not complying with societal norms—or nonsense, really.

Interestingly enough, Toni died in 1953 on the vernal equinox—a time when the day and night are equal in length and light and dark are in balance. The timing of her death is poetic because the Medial Archetype, this active and potent force in the psyche, is the very thing that helps us move between light and dark. It is the aspect within you that will show you how to mine the treasures of your Soul.

The dark holds the depths of the mystery and the hidden realm of all potential that lies in the mystery of the unknown. It is there, in that fruitful darkness, where we discover soulful nourishment and the vital importance of inner gazing—it is where we come to remember our light. Therein lies the journey of Medial Women, who can dance in the dark and return to the light more whole than before. Women like Toni Wolff who die on equinoxes. And yet the dance between light and dark still has more to teach us, so we journey to the shores of Japan, to the site of the Nomizo Falls and Kameiwa Cave, to dive into this small story of water and stone.

The Kameiwa Cave is a man-made cave created by civil engineers to allow the water from the nearby waterfall to flow well into the rice paddies that surround the area. When an equinox occurs, an optical illusion is created as the light moves through this cave, creating an image of a heart reflecting on the nearby water.

But the heart appears sideways, like so: ♥

In other words, if you go to this place, you have to turn your head to the right to fully see the image of the heart that appears in conjunction with the water and cave. Although many tourists are disappointed when they get there (because it only does this imagery "trick" at specific times, and they might not catch it), it is a good metaphor for the Medial Nature. **Even a man-made cavern of darkness can birth the heart of light under the right conditions.**

We may have to turn our heads (alter our perceptions) and arrive at the right time (on equinoxes or when the house is quiet) to see the heart of the image (the Spiritual understanding of the situation).

This surprising offering between nature and humanity offers us this reminder: It is when we move with balance between our inside and the outside worlds that we tend to the psychic waters that nurture our waking lives. Like water that flows healthily from the cave toward the rice paddies providing nourishment and harvest for many, we, too, can move in the same way to create beauty, abundance, and growth in our own lives. When the inside and outside work together, harmony is the result—*for everything.*

Your intuition guided by the Medial force will lead you through any dark tunnels where light is always assured. It is through Medial *movement* that we can use the insights of the heart and Soul to better our own lives and the world at large. In return, we give thanks to ancient and simple stories alike. Stories woven by the very nature that they describe, like water moving over stone, like all people are shaped by their time. Just like Toni Wolff, who wrote during distinctive times, World War II and later the Cold War. She was in many ways a woman of her time (aren't we all people of our times?), limited by external societal and gendered constraints but freer than many others. In fact, in her own work, she comments:

> Not every period offers optimal possibilities . . . but we cannot here go into all those historical, sociological, economic and religious causes which nowadays hamper the realization of the structural form inherent in a woman. A review of this kind would also be of little avail, since it could merely show by what factors the problem is determined. **What is of practical importance is the awareness of the existence of this problem, and the attempt to resolve the state of inner confusion by attaining greater consciousness.**[1]

So, let us lift our consciousness and perspective and pour light into Toni's work by moving the conversation forward. Simply because we live now, we have the advantage of a higher perspective. As such, we can grant her compassion for any errors that we think she made.

In fact, as I write these very words that you are reading, you may feel that there are errors in my opinions and in the way I write this story, and our grandchildren's children may one day look at them and see *severe* errors. And yet here I am, sharing my voice, as we all shine in the specific time-space realities that we find ourselves in. As a result, we should not be afraid to share our ideas and speak because of fear of perceived future judgment.

Let me address some things that we may notice in Toni's work: Nowadays, some may take issue with the gendered association of her structural analysis—she believed the female psyche was fundamentally different from a man's and thus wrote accordingly. She also didn't include any variation of a spectrum of gender identity, likely because the general cultural sentiment of her time was that biology and gender made a huge difference in how we perceived the world and how women (and everyone else) were treated as a result.

Rather than dwell on this, let's rise above the elements of separation and instead experience a crystalline flash of insight that helps us perceive every facet in the diamond and move into Spiritual sight. This form of sight holds the heart in every matter, meaning that when we come from a perspective of grace, unity, and compassion, we are led.

This is also where resonance comes in—it is the essence of a thing, not the name that matters most. In other words, it is *how you feel* in relation to the Medial essence—this dynamic force that matters most, not the words that I choose to use to explain this force. I will use many stories and metaphoric images to illuminate this higher and sacred force. Please stick with the stories and symbols that make your heart sing, as that is how you will know that you are close to the Medial nature. You will feel it.

Let me also clarify—I cannot definitively speak as to why Toni Wolff wrote in the feminine form, but I can speak for myself. I chose to write in the feminine form because this is how the Medial nature first appeared to me, so I write *her* in this way. For me, she is a facet, an image of the divine, and I write to express this sentiment. The Medial Woman is a fluid and dynamic force of nature, one that unites instead of divides, and she is available to *all people*. That said, though I will introduce you to many Medial Guides in many different ways—as women, men, and guardians of thresholds. You will come to learn over the course of this book that this Medial force does not remain static in one image or symbol. So please use whatever word and image that make you feel most comfortable. Here are some options for you: Medial, Medial Messenger, Medial Guide, Medial Archetype, Medial Nature, or Medial force. **If you "see" this force in an entirely different way, honor your own insights and afford room in your heart for other ways of seeing too.**

It is the essence that is important, not the label of identity. It is a way of connecting and being, a way of moving through the world. I'm not sure if Toni would agree (I imagine that she would, knowing what we know now), but I strongly feel that by virtue of this Medial Nature that anyone can connect and receive sacred insights and guidance.

The Medial force lives within and is activated when the person who embodies it *pays attention to unseen forces.* Toni's work stands today because she wrote about these ancient archetypal forces, forces that show us how the interconnected threads woven between the unseen and seen create this divine matrix we call reality. Forces that are so sacred and mysterious in nature that many people have dared to hone them into specific forms of identities and stories in an attempt to help make sense of what they are dealing with. Forces that seem to shapeshift with the times, but in reality, it is us as people who change with the times, and as a result we place new culturally fitting images onto these ancient forces. The stories, images, and names may change, but the force itself (its essence) remains the same. That Medial essence is within you and is destined to guide you.

For Toni, Medial Women (that is, women who embodied this force in their everyday lives) had social functions in their ancient societies. **They were the oracles, mediums, sibyls, medicine women, and dreamers in their communities.** Yet these Medials still exist today. They are also the parents who tend to their children with great inner knowing and compassion. They are the doulas who comfort those who are dying while greeting death as an old friend until their very own time comes. They are the herbalists who intuit nature's balm. They are the body workers who move energy. They are the analysts who sit patiently with their clients awaiting new life to emerge. They are the soulful creatives who birth beauty into the world. They are the ones who *know* without knowing how they know.

The repression and restriction of the Medial nature in society has caused an imbalance for us all. We need those who can whisper to nature. We need everyone who can see with the heart. We need everyone who can see with heart to pour compassion over every dark corner of their lives and then the world. We need those who can hear Spirit to listen, and we need the dreamers who can deliberately dream to shift reality. In other words, *we need you.*

At the same time, we also need the communities that will then listen to these whispers, these soulful understandings, and then act from this guidance. We need communities who understand that we need both the rational and intuitive to be in balance, like the sun and the moon, in order for us all to be balanced and well.

The shaman dreams for the community, the medicine woman heals, and the seer envisions the future. The Medial force is the instinct that moves between worlds. It is the very inner force that helps the shaman dream, the medicine woman heal, and the seer see. **The Medial Nature is the "personified" intrinsic force that bridges the unseen with the seen.** A conduit between worlds that allows healing and insight to take place for the highest good of all—no matter the healer, no matter the culture, and no matter the labels of identity. It is the direct link to the unseen worlds within each and every one of us.

Ideally, the community in turn then honors these sacred insights by taking care of those who provide them. It is bidirectional care held in balance by honoring one another's roles and purposes within the entire community. If the Medial force isn't honored in society; it is repressed, and then that is when we discover our collective shadow—whether we want to or not!

As a dream teacher, intuitive, and psychologist, I see many other Medials who are modern-day Cassandras, destined to give out accurate prophecies but who are bound to not be heard because their communities haven't placed any value on what they are saying. In these instances, the wisdom of the Soul has been replaced by the pursuit of sameness and logic. In turn, an individual who isn't being heard often becomes numb and ends up living and doing what they are told—to deny one's truth and as a consequence never live up to one's own potential! This causes a kind of inner death, a stifling of the heart, that suffocates life-giving creative forces. The vicious nature of it all is that then the community suffers even more. Both the individual and the community are pained when the Medial Nature is not honored.

Perhaps if Toni and I could sit down together and have tea, we could discuss these things. Maybe I'll dream on it one day. And in our discussion, I would bring her up to date with the world. I would tell her how the world is hurting and how pain and separation have become weapons of destruction. I would tell her that when I sit under a tree I hear the pleas of nature begging us to not just pay attention but to see things differently. (Many Spiritual teachers speak to this universal truth: When we change our perception, what we see changes in turn. And the time to practice this knowing is now!)

I would tell her that our one precious life is being wasted on distraction and that distraction is being fueled by the idea of separation. That there is an agenda behind that separation that has nothing to do with love and unity but everything to do with power. I believe that someone as close to the Medial Nature as Toni would understand, and I bet she would move the conversation even further forward if she were alive today. And so, I honor Toni and thank her for helping guide us Medials into the light.

In Toni's words, a woman is by nature conditioned by the Soul.[2] And in my words, we are all by nature conditioned by the Soul. Let us try to remember to live in this way.

CHAPTER 2

THE
THRESHOLD
OF
ENTRY

When my husband and I first moved to the East Coast, we didn't know anyone in our community. One of the first people to befriend us was an incredibly fun and kind eighty-four-year-old neighbor named Linda. She welcomed us with open arms and lighthearted connection, and before we knew it, we were visiting each other almost daily.

On one particular morning Linda showed me a birthday card that she bought for a soon-to-be-ninety-year-old friend of hers. On the front of the card was an image of a woman who looked incredibly regal and unbothered as she sat comfortably on a throne in a massive castle that looked quite foreboding. Inside of the card the tagline read: *Welcome to the other dark age*, and beneath those words, she had written *Happy Birthday, Queen*.

It's funny—mainly because the imagery and text are quirky but also because Linda is clearly a crone at the age of eighty-four, gifting this to a woman well older than her, both of them with their humor still intact. (May we all be so lucky!) She also happened to show me this card at the time of me writing this chapter, and it felt rather aligned, because the Medial

Nature tends to knock loudly on the psyche when people are beginning to hit middle age, around forty to fifty. *For many, these are the proverbial dark ages,* a stopping point that usually arrives quietly anticipated but often unannounced. Just like Linda and her friend, we can choose to own our thrones—to be "queens" of any transitional or "dark" time. For Linda, the dark that the card she was alluding to wasn't middle age but rather death—something she and her friend were addressing with humor and realism.

Through my own work and life, I have found that it is often during times of change when people begin to really listen to their Medial Nature. Understandably, during these times some people fall into crisis while others ebb and flow between the two responses. Some avoid confronting change altogether and stall as a consequence. Of course, there are also those who move through times of change with greater ease and knowing, surrendering to the wisdom of cycles far older than them.

Though our Medial Guide is always sending messages to us, it is generally during transitional times that people begin to listen. This is when people tend to accept the key to the royal interior castle. Why? Because they have finally learned that nothing external will ever fill the inner void caused by Soul abandonment or significant external loss. And by forty, most people have faced challenging things, like the loss of a loved one or the loss of a sacred dream that never came to be. Perhaps even a marriage or partnership that didn't work or even an exile from a place or home. Or simply the loss of realizing that time is in fact limited.

Loss comes wrapped in many guises, and although we can likely all trace small losses throughout our lives (like a loss of a belief, a friendship, attractiveness, or a goal), it is usually the big, jarring losses that force us to listen. It is then when we must turn inward for greater depth of understanding—it is then that we must meet our own Medial Natures directly.

Loss evokes intense grief, and sometimes it is so difficult that it can feel like a canyon is being created within your own heart. It takes Spiritual maturity to hold the duality of life, to experience change, endings, and death, and to still choose to consciously move forward with levity. It takes courage to build a bridge over that canyon in your heart and to actively allow life and joy back in after grief has ripped it into two. The silver lining here—perhaps like the shiny appearance of graying hair—is that it is in those times of change and transition when we can often hear our own Medial Natures best. It is when we are "lost" or in the "dark," in the pit of grief and despair, or facing unwanted change that we can meet her and ourselves more fully and directly.

The Medial Nature awakens when we begin to authentically ask the big questions, and it's usually discomfort that evokes these questions:

Why are we here? What does this life mean? Is there life after this? What is my Soul? Where is my Soul? Why did this change or tragedy happen? Have I been wise about the choices I've made? Am I wise with how I use my time?

It is through asking these questions that our intrinsic connection to the archetypal Medial Woman is activated within because the Medial Nature is, and has always been, rooted in two worlds—the world of the mundane and the world of Soul. In fact, the very word *medial* implies middle, medium, centered, mediator. It is the middle path of remembrance: one foot here, one foot elsewhere. The art of living in a balanced manner no matter what arises in our realities, and equally the art of calling in balance in an unhinged world.

In many ways, it is unsurprising that we may answer the call of the Medial Woman at middle age. As I've mentioned, she is always calling, but for many this is the time that they actually answer her call because the kids are older, and life has changed, and the old ways of dealing are simply not working anymore. Often grief is the initiation that returns us to our heart home and aging is one of the gateways for that initiation.

That said, there are really no prescriptive deadlines, circumstances, or ages that can contain the Medial Nature. It is impossible to contain the Medial Woman in an age, time, or space. As the late master mythologist Joseph Campbell so eloquently shared with us in *Mythic Worlds, Modern Words*, "Time and space are gone in the enchantment of the heart."[1] And that is exactly where we find the Medial Nature—in *the enchantment of our own hearts. At any age.*

We can see this so clearly when we watch children play, as they are naturally close to this sacred enchantment. How many children do you know that have imaginary friends? Psychologically speaking, we could say that imaginary friends are personalized externalized aspects of the child's psyche, and although this is true in many circumstances, we must afford the possibility that many children are simply interacting with the *unseen world*, that they are using their very own Medial Natures to interact with Spirit and the greater nonphysical aspects of reality. My brief interpretation is that perhaps children can experience both realities at the same time. So, there is an imaginary friend that is psychological in nature, and there is a Spiritual friend too. I know that some people may disagree with me on this point, but we must be able to entertain possibilities that aren't just about the "seen" world. We don't live in just an all-or-nothing reality; we live in a Medial reality, where it can be both "this" *and* "that" where Spirit and the imaginal exist in relation to one another. In my experience children are often naturally in harmony with this dual reality even if the adults around them aren't. Often, this multidimensional reality is what we have to relearn to perceive as adults in order to restore well-being. We may have to resuscitate both our imaginal worlds and our connection to Spirit in order to see our lives and place in this world more accurately.

I have been close to the Medial Nature my whole life. I think it's largely because I spent so much time in the wild outdoors as a young child, lying on the grass or climbing trees and singing songs to the sky. Being close to nature helps one to become a clear channel. It is a primal connection, one so ancient that when I lie on the grass now, I can hear our great mother speak. But for a long time, I felt like I had lost that connection. I felt isolated from a life-giving force that I couldn't name but knew existed, mainly because I was spending too much time physically indoors or in the confines of my own mind. Perhaps you've experienced that too. The mind can be a prison or a place of expansion, and how we wield our awareness is what we will experience. If we are closed off to awe then we cannot perceive it even if it is right there in front of us.

In relation to this, I once saw a young girl playing in a park who was in such a state of contented bliss. She was running and singing, and after a while she stopped to catch butterflies. She managed to catch one in her open hands. As she carefully released this butterfly back into the wild, she squealed, as young children often do, and then she screamed the words, "Good luck!" In response, her mother asked her why she had said that, and she in turn told her in a cute but matter-of-fact tone, "Oh, silly, because he needed it."

As adults, it is often our innocence, our core nature of goodness that gets tainted by life experiences. Loss, trauma, overtly rigid belief structures, constricting and repetitive thoughts, politics, broken hearts—all these things can seemingly wear down the belief in the goodness of self and other people. This fracturing begs you to consider: Can you come back to innocence when it feels like life has knocked you down? Will you become bitter or free in the face of all those big and small hardships and losses? Will you choose to return to love even when love has been taken from you? Will you rise from your suffering and those self-created cages around your heart and be a beacon of light for all?

When we return to the Medial Nature, we return to a path of innocence—but it is not childish or naive. It is not like a child chasing butterflies. It is an innocence that holds a return to the heart's wisdom. *It is a way of consciously being in contact with that which is unbreakable, the core of who we are, the sacred heart and Soul center of everything. It is the innocence of our true Spiritual natures and choosing to move through life from this wise and whole place. Ultimately, it is choosing over and over again to operate from one's heart center in order to be in an energetic alignment with the experiences that evoke awe and connection.*

Let us now journey into story.

In Ireland, in a medieval town called Carlingford, there is a site that holds Long Woman's Grave. If you travel to see it, you will find a headstone with her story inscribed upon it. Although some say that it is entirely fictional, like all good stories and myth, it reminds us of what is so easy to forget. So the story goes:

Two Irish brothers of noble stature are to divide the land upon their father's death, the beloved ruler of Omeath. One brother, more cunning than the other, decides to trick his brother, and in doing so, steals his share of the land. In his slyness, he tells his brother that he can have all the land "as far as he can see." But when it comes down to the day of "seeing," the land is mostly covered by mist and cloud. As a result, the now-poor brother is simply left with one mountain and ravine—nature's hollow.

Yet all is not lost, as the unfortunate brother still owns a ship, and so he sets sail for foreign seas. He becomes rich from his travels, and on arriving in Spain one fine day, he happens to save a noble man and his daughter from peril. Romance blossoms from this fortuitous stroke of fate! The noble man and woman fall in love and marry, and so he begins to tell her great tales of Omeath. Lured in by great fortunes and land as far as the eye can see, the noble wife agrees to leave her true home for the land of Omeath.

Her husband, as promised, takes her to the same ravine, to nature's hollow, and whispers these words to her: "Our land for as far as the eye can see." Yet the mist remains, and our noble wife, so disappointed by what she sees, and having left her true home behind, dies right there on that very spot. Her body falls deep into the ravine—nature's hollow.

In response, her grief-stricken husband, so disgusted with his own duplicity, kills himself by leaping into a deep dark pond at the edge of a crossroad. So, too, does our tale end with a descent—a long grave of hollow, of disappointment, as both husband and wife are now dead.

A naive heart like that of our noble woman, who cannot see danger coming, is not the same as the strong heart of a Medial Woman. A Medial Woman avoids traps because she knows better. She can peer into the imaginal future as if it is a crystal ball and see potential pitfalls before she acts. She does not get fooled by false gold and shiny trimmings. And she does not get lured in by tales of Omeath because her instincts are sharp, and her intuitive sight is keen. She trusts her Medial Nature, her true home (her Spiritual center), and from this place she makes wise choices.

In our modern times, we can see this playing out in other ways. A Medial does not run back to an ex to play out a familial pattern of rejection and abandonment, or simply because they are afraid of being alone. They do not abandon themselves through playing out patterns of self-sabotage. Psychological and ancestral patterns of heartache are put down because they are brave enough to step into the dark unknown in order to live out something different for themselves and in many ways for the lineage before and ahead of them. A Medial also knows when to pick up their wounded heart and move on after life has taken something precious from them, though through no fault of their own, like in times of death.

We now look to the husband to learn from this cautionary tale. Here we are advised not to be fooled by quick words, unsavory hearts, and empty promises. We learn to not be misled by those who wish us harm, and in return not to make empty promises ourselves if we have been fooled. Overpromising and underdelivering (that is, living through ego) will cause severe heartache and pain for oneself and others if it is allowed. And at the crossroad of death, one does not want to be disappointed by one's own life choices. We do not want to lie in a deep dark marsh of regret at the crossroad point between life and death.

It is important to act with integrity, and it is okay to come home empty-handed at times. It's okay to speak the truth. It is okay to lose sometimes, to have less gold, less material hoopla. Who is truly impressed by all these things? The noble woman who wants it all but who ends up dead from disappointment. If this story resonates with you, it may be time to release any inner or outer deception and any excessive material competitiveness simply in order to return to an inner state of peace. In other words, heartfelt innocence. Equally, this isn't to say that you can't have nice things or be abundant; it is simply to bring any material excess or desire back into balance.

If this conflict is within you (where you feel pushed and pulled by wanting and not having), pour honey on what you feel is lacking in the hollows and ravines of your own life. Grieve when you need to and then breathe gratitude into every good thing that you do have. True abundance creates a vortex of flourishment for all, and it is often created through the Medial heart. In our Spiritual homes, our hearts, the land extends as far as the eye can see. When we remember this universal truth, we can tap into that high vibration (a state of inner serenity and security) and create abundance in the here and now in so many ways.

We can always return to well-being and love; we simply need to *choose* to do so. It takes effort. We need to put down the past, release the burden of loss, and reenter into a dialogue with our own Medial and soulful natures. Let yourself lie on the grass and allow any grief and tales of wrongdoing to simply seep down into the earth. Let your grief move through the earth until it is made of dirt and not stone. Do anything, but do not become closed off, otherwise life becomes like a living grave, one in which you bury yourself long before your time, because nobody, but nobody, wants to wind up in a long grave in nature's hollow!

Now, I return to thoughts of my neighbor Linda, who, at the tender age of eighty-four, is still laughing as she tells me she has one foot in her grave. Death may very well be around the corner for her, but for now she is too busy living to be severely bothered by it. She is still laughing, exercising, going out with friends, and allowing life to be for the simple joys that can still be had. We drink champagne on the porch and drive together to the oncologist. Life is wild in its duality, and through it all, her Medial heart remains open.

Let us also be under no illusion this does not happen accidentally; it is because she wills it so. Linda has many physical aches and pains: She buried two husbands, and she lost a father to war. These are just to name a few of the hardships she has overcome. Yet none of these things permanently closed her heart at any point during her life. She is full of love, life, and playful innocence, but like any good crone, she is also discerning and wise. She leans into her intuitive knowing daily. She is a Medial—a crone of knowing, a Wild woman in her eighties. She is all these things, and I feel incredibly grateful to have met her.

CHAPTER 3

MEDIATRIX *OF* ALL GRACES

Some five hundred years ago in what is now Mexico City, a farmer named Juan Diego is on his morning walk. As he walks, I imagine him doing what he does most mornings: going through the motions while mulling over his thoughts. Yet a humble man connected to nature often finds unanticipated treasures, and on this particular morning, Juan is about to meet a Medial treasure.

At the top of the Tepeyac hill Juan suddenly finds himself in an extraordinary situation when an apparition suddenly appears in front of him. A woman of Spirit cloaked in light tells him that she would like a sanctuary to be built so that she can bestow her love, protection, and compassion to all who come to her. Juan is so moved by this vision that he finds the local archbishop and tells him about what he has experienced. Although the bishop listens to Juan, he simply does not believe his story.

The Lady of the Hill reappears, and this time Juan speaks to her, and he tells her that perhaps she's made a mistake in choosing him to convey her message. Wouldn't it be easier to convince the bishop if the message was delivered through a man of stature? She in turn responds that she has made no error and that he must move forward with confidence. He must go to the bishop and tell him that she is the Virgin Mother Mary, the Mother of God, and that she requests a space for her children to come and speak with her.

Juan returns to the bishop, who graciously listens but who still does not believe him. Yet this time he tells Juan that if she is really the Mother of God, she should send a sign. In other words, he requests proof of validity. Now, our farmer has a regular life, and although he has had quite a transformative experience, he needs to tend to some earthly matters that don't involve being the go-between for the sacred mystery and a religious order.

Unfortunately, Juan's uncle has fallen gravely ill and has requested that he travel to a nearby town so that he can find a priest who can come back to hear his confession. Juan wishes to honor his uncle's request, and so he sets off. On his journey, he decides to avoid going up the hill in case he gets caught up by the Lady of the Hill and is delayed in helping his uncle. Yet his detour is proven futile as she finds him anyway, and as the story goes, this is what she imparts to him:

> Listen and understand, my humblest son. There is nothing to frighten and distress you. Do not let your heart be troubled, and let nothing upset you. Is it not I, your Mother, who is here? Are you not under my protection? Are you not, fortunately, in my care? Do not let your uncle's illness distress you. It is certain that he has already been cured. Go up to the hilltop, my son, where you will find flowers of various kinds. Cut them, and bring them into my presence.[1]

Juan journeys to the top of the hill once again, and he is astounded to find Castilian roses blooming in the peak of winter. And so, he gathers some roses and places them carefully in his robe, honoring the Lady of the Hill, who has reappeared once again. He then walks slowly down the hill with his robe full of roses and goes to see the bishop.

In the presence of the bishop and clergy members, he unfurls his robe. As he does, the roses fall to the floor and an image of the Lady of the Hill miraculously appears in full color on his robe for everyone to see. The bishop and his men fall down to their knees in astonishment—the miraculous sign has been delivered and received for all to see.

This is the story of the Lady of Guadalupe, the patron saint of Mexico, who is also known as Mother Mary, Mediatrix of All Graces. **She is a Medial Woman, a mediatrix, who promises to pour divine grace upon those who invoke her.**

Toni Wolff makes a distinction between a Medial Woman and a Mediatrix, and what she comes to say is that a Mediatrix is the most empowered version of the Medial Woman. This is a concept that we will briefly explore together later, when we discuss the shadow side of what it means to be Medial.

The Medial Woman has many names—the sacred principle often does as it is cloaked in the Spirit of its times—yet her essence is almost always the same: She is a mediator; a messenger of divine grace, and she is one with supernatural grace. **That is, she delivers messages, grace, miracles, love, and healing to those who petition her.** Here are some of her previous and current names: Mother Mary, Mediatrix of All Graces; Our Lady of Guadalupe; Queen of Heaven; Mother of Miracles; Charites; Lady of the Hill; Lady of the Heavens; Mother Night; Our One True Mediator; Fierce Lady of the Immaculate Heart; and Our Great Mother of Mysteries.

Now, let me preface this by saying that I am not a particularly religious person, but I am very Spiritually orientated, finding the sacred in many ways, and so discovering the connection between the Medial Woman, the Mediatrix, and the Lady of Guadalupe in a more traditional sense has been filled with many surprising and wonderful *aha* moments. That said, what I want to share with you now is not a religious overview of our Lady of Guadalupe, but rather a *symbolic look* at her through the lens of the Medial archetype: an aspect within us all that can both receive and extend divine grace.

Let us now return to Juan. Here we have our humble farmer and we learn that humility and humbleness are two of his greatest assets in this extraordinary situation. It is what helps facilitate a dialogue with the Mediatrix of Divine Grace or the Lady of the Hill. The word *humility* in our modern times can sound a bit off-kilter, but what I am speaking about here is not about walking on your knees as a supplicant, but rather being free of arrogance and pride. In other words, it is not an overinflated ego that hears and sees Spirit. It is when ego is put aside that divine grace can flow through. Ultimately, a receptive channel is most clear when the mind can find stillness among egoic thoughts and desires. This, I believe, is true for all of us.

Juan even petitions the Lady of the Hill to find someone better suited for the job than he. Yet her direction to him is to be confident in delivering her message. Here we see that humility is not to be confused for meekness. It takes courage, confidence, and strength to hear and deliver messages of divine grace when you do not feel ready. Even though our dear Juan feels unprepared, he does as he requested. He moves beyond his fears despite his concerns, and he goes and petitions the bishop with confidence.

The bishop still does not believe him, but this time, something tells him to investigate—so he asks for a sign as proof of validity. This is an act of faith, as well as a test. It is a handing over to a higher power, and so we can see that this is a type of turning point in our story. When we hand over power and request direction, "proof," a sign, we have entered into commune with higher forces. We open the door to infinite possibility through handing "it" over. For many, it is also a test of one's own capacity for faith in the impossible. If you are testing the Universe/Spirit by asking for a sign, you are at the same time testing your ability to receive it.

At this turning point, Juan is also confronted with some very everyday realities. His uncle is very ill, and he has requested a favor from him, which is for Juan to travel to the nearby town in order to find a priest so that he can tell his confession. Juan wants to honor his uncle but worries that he will be delayed by the Lady of the Hill, so he tries to avoid her by going around the hill instead. His heart is still full of good intentions, and yet she still finds him, and instead of delaying him, she consoles him.

This is key: You can run away from divine grace, you can detour, take the longer route, think the mundane is more important, difficult, and fixed, but divine grace will *always* find you. Here I hear people retorting that "real problems require real solutions." Our story tells us that real problems can be solved in an instant with divine grace. Her voice adapted says:

"Hear me on this: Do not let your heart be troubled and let nothing upset you. Am I not here? Are you not under my protection? Are you not in my care? Do not let your problems overwhelm you. It is certain that they have already been resolved. Go up to the hilltop, where you will find flowers, and bring them into my presence."

We learn that we can meet the feminine principle at the hilltop of a higher perspective, where we are gifted access to the sacred rose mysteries. Mysteries that can bring you into alignment with divine grace, which can create miracles. We are also shown that reality can be shifted in an instant with divine grace. In other words, miracles can happen fast. In fact, in a crisis, don't run to the other town; go to the hill (gain a clear and higher perspective) and commune with divine grace. In other words, use your Medial Nature to see things from a higher perspective and ask for help. Perhaps then the problem that brought you there in the first place will instantly be resolved on your behalf.

Another message hidden within this story is that of the symbolic union between the bishop of the church and the Lady of the Hill. If we look at the bishop and the lady, we can see that they are a symbolic pair of opposites. **These opposites exist internally within us, and they equally exist out in the real world.** The bishop represents Logos, structure, the rational, or the laws of the sacred—he requires proof and validity. The Lady of the Hill represents the divine grace, the intuitive aspects of self, and the mysterious aspects of the sacred. Juan brings the two together—he is our Medial man in this story—he is the mediator, the bridge, the connector between divine grace and sacred order, the messenger who receives divine grace and shares it with others. After all, it is Juan who delivers the Lady of the Hill's message to the bishop.

Once the bishop and the Lady of the Hill are united (that is, they come into symbolic contact with each other), something incredible occurs: a Spiritual and physical lighthouse, or basilica, is built.

Now, the Basilica of Guadalupe is a pilgrimage site in Mexico that sees millions of seekers come to it.[2] It is a beacon of hope for many. Without the bishop or the lady of the hill, this lighthouse would not have been created. It also would not have been created had Juan failed to connect the two "opposites" together. Had he failed to mediate their connection with his own Medial Nature. So, in the end of this experience, we beautifully witness an integration and harmonizing of the intuitive and the rational, the physical and the Spiritual, the masculine and the feminine, both in our symbolic story and in reality. In other words, things are held in balance—they are in harmony, and for the time being, nothing else needs to be done at this point, as stasis has occurred.

Analytically, we could say:

When two opposites exist, a transcendental third naturally appears, which brings all three into harmony. A pair of opposites can be brought into harmony by a mediator that sits in the center, and equilibrium for all three will be felt as a result. Here's another way of thinking about this: The Left Path and the Right Path are a pair of opposites. The third symbol that appears then is the Middle Path (without the left or right, the middle could not exist). None of the paths cease to exist. Rather, all three exist simultaneously and can be brought into harmony when the mediator-connector principle unites them together.

We see another clear example of this in tarot in the card of the High Priestess. On the image of the card, we see a woman who is a priestess (a channel for the sacred) who is seated between two pillars positioned on either side of her. One pillar is black and the other is white. In the image, the High Priestess is the third symbol—she is the middle path—who lives and exists between the two black and white pillars. She is both the mediator and connector principle (a Medial woman) that unites the two opposites. Thus, all three symbols are in unison and harmony. In the card's image, you will also notice that the two pillars are rigid and stationary, whereas the priestess is fluid and free—her robe looks like flowing water, and through this we can understand that she is ethereal in her ability to Medially move and adapt.

In other words, by activating your Medial Nature and then acting from that centered place, you can bring two opposites into balance. You can be the mediator and connector who sits between the two extremes. **If you do this, you will then be able to move and flow between polarities easily, and you will also be able to instinctively map the path ahead.** This is an incredibly helpful skill to have in a world that is changing faster than you can read these words.

The middle path would not be a middle path without the two diverging opposites on either side of it. If there was just one path, it would be *the* path. Yet we live in a world of duality, and we see this so clearly in our lived experiences. Opposites are everywhere, and yet contrast in itself is not a problem. It is how we choose to approach contrast that either becomes problematic or harmonic. Our collective and individual intention makes all the difference in harmonizing or obliterating balance.

It is also worth noting that it is often through contrast that we expand in consciousness.

Ultimately, a Medial journey is a sacred initiation. It is an initiation of the heart that asks you to release yourself from the bonds of the mind—that is, the story of what is deemed absolutely right or wrong by the ego of self or the ego of others. Instead, you are asked to open your heart up to divine grace and move through life from this place, to see the future, present, and past from this place. **You are asked to stand centered in a world of extremes, emanating strength and compassion while holding duality in balance. When you reflect balance from within, it then becomes a mirror for others in the real world. You shift reality when you unite the internal with the external through the pathway of the heart.**

Returning now to our story of the bishop and the Lady of Guadalupe, we discover that the heart should also stand at the epicenter of reason and structure (or Logos). The Lady of Guadalupe stands at the heart of the basilica. She is the heart of the church. So, we once again learn that our hearts should be at the center of our reason and logic. Our hearts should also be at the center of any structures that we build. A heart that sits at the center of reason and logic leads to action forged from compassion and forgiveness. This is what produces harmony.

A simple way of embodying this is by imagining that the basilica is within you, the bishop is within you, Juan is within you, our Lady is within you, and that the pilgrimage seeker is also within you. How can you bring all these symbolic figures into balance?

To do this, first identify who you would most likely be, and then imagine yourself as every other person instead, rather than just jumping to that one figure. What does it feel like to be the bishop? What does it feel like to be the basilica? The pilgrim? Juan? The Mediatrix? Are you a pilgrim seeking a lighthouse, a sanctuary that you have to journey to? Could it already be within you, or do you need to go out and build one in the world?

Once you've placed yourself in many identities, divergent aspects of self can naturally unify, as you are seeing them through a higher sort of sight: You are seeing them through the eyes of love and compassion. From this perspective, all symbolic figures live calmly within you. Equally, if you find yourself in fierce disagreement with other people or "figures," make your heart the epicenter of your reason and logic where compassion leads first, and then see if they can meet you there.

This simple exercise can also bring up any implicit biases or judgments that you have regarding specific symbolic figures. If you have a very strong reaction to one of the key figures in the story, then that is the very person you should focus your attention on. Ask yourself: Why do I feel so uncomfortable here? Every single person who appears in your life and vortex, as well as any symbolic figure within you, has a sacred purpose, and it is up to you to see the connection, even if that connection is of a collective nature as opposed to a personal one.

Although the Lady of Guadalupe is not just a symbolic story, if we look at her in this way, we can feel close to her without needing to travel anywhere. She can be invoked *within* us. The Medial Woman, the Mediatrix of All Graces, or the Lady of the Hill can appear to us—to you. She can be petitioned and will extend divine grace. **Through this symbolic retelling, we have also learned that we can extend divine grace through our own Medial Natures. By allowing our hearts to be at the center of our reasoning, we can thrive in miraculous ways.**

At this point, many people often ask: Why did the Lady of Guadalupe not just *appear* to the bishop? Because this story teaches us about *the initiation of the heart*. The initiation of our own humble and powerful hearts. Being privy to divine grace requires a pure heart exactly like children's stories teach us—a heart of gold. Juan is the mediator and the connector in this story. He acts as the messenger between divine grace and sacred order, and he is successful in this because he is pure in heart. Had the Lady of the Hill gone straight to the bishop, we would also have been at a loss to understand that divine grace is available to all of us—"even" to a humble man like Juan. Stature or titles have nothing to do with Spiritual connection and divine grace—these sacred things are available to everyone.

Ultimately, if we strip the symbols and titles of *the bishop*, *the Lady*, and *Juan* from this narrative and simply distill the message down to its core essence, this is what we are left with: **A pure heart is a Medial heart. It is the tool that allows us to receive and extend divine grace, and with divine grace, anything is possible. Miracles are a by-product of graceful union.**

It is the heart that mediates divine grace and order. It is your very own heart that can and will bridge the mystery and the mundane if you choose to move through this initiation. Equally, without mind, heart, and Soul, there can be no harmony and balance in a world of duality, which means that it is up to each and every one of us to activate our sacred hearts. It is up to you! Especially when the world is knocking you around or when the collective atmosphere is frightening. The cure for fragmentation is to return to the sacred heart over and over again until this state of grace is the unifying force that is activated between opposites.

So, what exactly is the sacred heart?

The sacred heart is when the individual heart meets with the cosmic heart, where division dissolves into everythingness. It is in the Medial place, the sacred middle, where divine grace meets humanity. It is from this place where miracles can be petitioned and where divine messages can easily be received. This is available to you.

If you activate your center—your heart—you will come into contact with divine grace. You will then become an embodied Medial messenger: a bridge between the heavenly and the earthly. This means that you can receive Spiritual insight and guidance that is supremely positive and helpful for both you and the collective. You can also mediate divine grace and connect others to it. You are then a mediator of divine grace, a Medial, who acts from a place of compassion—because you are connected to a larger Mediatrix of divine grace. Your sacred heart is wide open—the channel is clear. Ultimately, divine grace cannot be locked into one place; it cannot be controlled or coerced, just as the Lady of Guadalupe cannot be forced or contained within any one building. Just as Juan tries to avoid her by going around the hill, divine grace can and will appear anywhere.

If grace is housed somewhere, it is because it chooses to be there.

Our own connection to divine grace is absolutely incorruptible, and through connecting to it via your Medial Nature, your life can absolutely turn around in many miraculous ways. It is also through divine grace that we can come to learn to perceive the world in a better way. Ultimately, it is when we choose to see through the eyes of divine grace that reality can change for the better.

Now, what does it mean to see through the eyes of divine grace?

It means to reflect on the concept of forgiveness. To ask: Who has forgiven you, and who do you need to forgive? Who has extended mercy to you, and who do you need to extend mercy to? I can think of so many people who have afforded me grace or second chances and greater understanding when I was in fear, in pain, and simply foolish or hyper-egoic because of my fallible humanness. Yet receiving and offering empathy frees us from perpetuating pain and suffering. It extends grace to us all.

As the great Martin Luther King, Jr., taught, "I have also decided to stick with love ... Hate is too great a burden to bear."[3] Divine grace has also taught me that hate is too great a burden to bear, so I practice extending forgiveness to those who have caused me harm (I come from a lineage of war survivors, and with that comes many layers of trauma). Hate just breeds more hate, and compassion for self and others just releases everyone from the victim/perpetrator cycle. The middle point exists, and through it we can transcend extremes. It is a return to the heart regardless of external structures and demands. There will always be those who fall into a lower level of consciousness that is focused on violence or hate, but if many mediators and seekers come together, their influence can greatly affect the external. So, if you find yourself feeling rigid and stuck in a way of thinking that is causing you or others distress, then perhaps the following words, which are inspired by the poet and mystic Rumi, are for you: *In the field of dreams, where our Souls lay down, we hear the heartbeat of unity through our Medial ears. Beyond the ideas of wrongdoing and rightdoing, the phrase* each other *doesn't make sense because* we are one with one another and all that is. *The Soul is our experience, our awareness is the key, and the dream field is available to us at any time.*

When you drop into the heart, your center, you have the opportunity to look and listen with your *Spiritual* eyes and ears. That is your second sight and hearing. You look inside for guidance (*in*sight), and you hear with your Spiritual ears. In this instance, the instruction is offered up in the very word itself: *heart*. In other words, hear with your heart! Listen to others with kindness and extend kindness out. It will be returned.

Out beyond debated ideas of wrongdoing and rightdoing, in the field of dreams, Medials are required to return to earth to remind others to meet in the middle. A path of equanimity: a field that can be created in the here and now, our modern-day reality, where we all claim, "I am not your enemy, and you are not mine. I am no one's victim, and I victimize no one." From this space, love permeates the fabric of our existence, and balance is an inevitability as we sit gracefully between two extremes. Solutions then arise from the sacred center of higher consciousness. As a group, we then become thrivers of our own collective consciousness as opposed to survivors of it.

We find ourselves in groups in many ways: our families, partnerships, cultures, countries, and even work environments. Any interpersonal dynamic or collective dynamic that is polarized by severe contrast can be brought into greater harmony by both sides meeting in the middle. One can hold good boundaries and still remain empathetic—it does not need to be one over the other. We are all fallible because we are human.

It is so easy to fall into dichotomous thinking: where it's all "good" or all "bad" *or* entirely "this" or "that" (these are examples of cognitive distortions or thinking errors delineated by cognitive behavioral therapy creator Dr. Aaron T. Beck). But we must bring back Spiritual maturity into the conversation. We must forgive ourselves and extend compassion outward toward one another just like our wise Mediatrix of All Graces—we must keep our hearts open at all costs. Anything that seeks to divide on the illusion of differences is not coming from the heart. Spirit knows no agenda like this. May we all recognize the sacred within and without us, as there is ample room for us all to thrive. May we also know in our hearts that compassion reduces suffering in the world and within ourselves and then embody this with our actions. Let us now turn our attention away from the collective and toward the path of personal transformation as you come to discover a new mythic journey.

CHAPTER 4

THE MEDIAL WOMAN'S MYTHIC JOURNEY OF INITIATION

We have been dancing around the edges of the Medial Woman up until this very moment. I have whispered tales gentle in nature and offered you a soft skeleton, the base bones of stories that outline her shape, and like skeleton woman herself, bone by bone, she must come back. Perhaps you've heard that sound before, the creaking of an old floor, or was that an old woman? It's hard to tell. Like a poor selkie washed up onshore, she's all skin and bones, taught to be tame by those who love her but who cannot allow her back to her true home. Yet, as we've seen, one can never contain her, lock her tightly into one tale or abode.

She is vast like the ocean, wild and deep, and she is always on time.

And now she is here as an answer for these times, a Medial medicine maker who can breathe life back into wild bones, and when she is done, she will return once more into the abyss, where her true heart belongs. She will run for the sea and then leap, just as you will when you set yourself free.

So, listen now with acute hearing as we stand on the shoulders of a strong woman, Clarissa Pinkola Estés, a Wild Medial, who gifted us these words:

"Bone by bone, hair by hair, Wild Woman comes back. Through night dreams, through events half understood and half remembered, Wild Woman comes back. She comes back through story."[1]

And story we shall tell, and as you will come to see that these two sisters, both Medial and Wild, were once split at birth. But like any good pair, they can never be truly torn apart: Not even death can separate them. Like stars and the sky, they are a constellation—a double face of one moon, or soul. And as sister seers, they are the archetype of our times: an Instinctual pair that make us whole.

So, listen now, sweet reader, breathe in deep, as you are about to meet the Wild Medial within. She belongs to you, and you belong to her. And yet in order to find her, we must not just sing her flesh back onto our bones,[2] but we must discover and use our own magic. Not just through words or a social media retelling, but through an actual practice. The very ritual that is our life, especially now, as we dance at the edge of collective destruction—or was that rebirth. And as she tells me: Time won't tell this ending; we will.

And so, our story now begins with a blue bird, and through her song, we see our two sisters. Where the Medial meets the Wild and once again becomes whole, this ancient Slavic tale is now retold.

GO I KNOW NOT WHERE AND BRING BACK I KNOW NOT WHAT

Like many good stories that begin just before dawn, we enter a rich tale filled with kings and queens and a royal sharpshooter named Fedot.[3] It's a long story, so settle in as we travel with our sharpshooter as he enters into the deep dark forest—a place he visits often on his hunts for the king. Although the woods are familiar to him on this very morning, he sees something rare: a magnificent bird, a blue dove.

Now, this blue dove is a bird of passage, a true traverser of faraway places as she migrates to and from distant lands. And although she is magnificent, he is a royal hunter, and so he takes his shot and injures her so. But just before he has time to wring her little neck, she speaks to him in a human voice, a coo of wonder that weeps:

"Please! Please, don't kill me! Take me home, rest me on the window's edge, and let me sleep, and as I drift into slumber, strike me with the back of your hand, and you will gain great fortune!"

It's not every day that you hear a blue dove speak, so our royal hunter does as he is asked. One soft strike later, he is astounded to find that the bird has now turned into a woman of immense beauty. In fact, our blue dove fell flat on the floor and became a Soul-maiden almost too beautiful to be imagined or even described. What luck!

After some time, Blue Dove declares to Fedot, "In truth, I am not a blue dove. I am a king's daughter. You have known how to get me. Now know how to live with me. You will be my husband, and I will be your wife." And so they marry and love each other.

Yet over time, she sees her husband working so very hard, each hunt an endeavor, so she whispers to him:

"My dear love, the hunt is so demanding for you. Go and borrow some money. One or two hundred rubles will do, and when you have it, go and buy some silk with the money." The sharpshooter follows through and buys the silk, but now he is beginning to feel a bit shaky about the whole situation, so she tells him to go to sleep. "Rest easy, my love, and in the morning, all things shall be the wiser."

And when he is deep in slumber, she goes out and stands under the vast night sky. And it is there where she opens her magic book, and as she does, two youths appear from it who say, "What is it that you wish, Soul bird? Tell us so."

Now our beautiful wife with the heart of a dove responds in kind:

"Take this silk and wield it so. Make it that it may become the most beautiful tapestry in all the land. Let all the images of the king's domain be set upon it, and do this within the hour."

In 10 minutes, the tapestry is completed. And now at her feet lies the most beautiful image woven of silk and magic, made into matter in the middle of the night by two youths who simply disappear back into the ether of her magic book.

The morning comes, and she tells her husband to go to the market to sell it, but there is one thing she tells him that he must not do, and that is set a price for the tapestry; instead, they must come to him with a value. The merchants at the market revel in its beauty, as such a thing has rarely been seen. They haggle and talk. Finally, a steward of the king ends the commotion when he bids an astounding 10,000 rubles. The steward then takes the tapestry to the king, who sees it and in return offers him 25,000 rubles!

The king's steward is so happy with his financial return that he sets off for the sharpshooter's house to see if he can get another tapestry, and that is when he sees her—Blue Dove! She is so beautiful—in fact, beyond beauty—that he falls in love with her right then and there. Dark thoughts begin to cloud his mind: *Why should a simple sharpshooter have such a lovely wife? She should be mine! I am closer to the king; I am a man of higher stature.*

Now madly in love and consumed by wanting her, he returns to the equally wifeless king, who notices a significant change in the steward. At once, he demands to know what has happened, and the steward tells him of the exquisiteness of the sharpshooter's wife. Such is the king in his power that he decides that such a precious thing should be his and his alone. Dark thoughts cloud his mind again.

And so, he commands that the steward conspires to be rid of Fedot—and if he does not succeed, it will be the gallows of death for him. The steward, now steeped in grief and panic, tries to hatch up a plan. He walks and walks and somehow finds himself on backward roads and wasted places when he comes upon a stranger—Baba Yaga.

A twisted witch, some may say, but on each day she does decide what and who she is. And on this day, she simply says:

"I know your woes, dear steward, and I will help you. Tell the king to send the sharpshooter to the thirteenth kingdom. In that kingdom is an island, and on that island, there is a deer with golden antlers. Tell him to catch that deer—near impossible—and all your problems will be solved."

The steward thanks her with gold and then goes to tell the king his plan, and so our tale further unfolds.

Fedot is told the news and must go to the 13th kingdom, as the king's word is final. And so Blue Dove once again seeks to help her husband by ushering him into a gentle sleep. She goes outside and calls on her magic book. The two youths reappear, and she tells them to bring the deer that lives in the farthest kingdom in the 13th land. And in a flash, they return with it in tow.

Once again, morning arrives wiser than the night before, and she shows her husband the deer. "Take it on the ship with you, hide it from the crew, and after the sixth day, turn around, set sail for the shore, and when you are ready, show the king."

So, Fedot, our faithful husband, does as he is advised and a week later returns from sea with the deer in hand. "Impossible," the king shouts. "This trip was supposed to take his life. How did this happen?" And so, the king is forced to send Fedot home.

In turn, the steward is now in severe trouble as the king unleashes all his frustration and rage upon him and tells him to dispose of the sharpshooter one more time . . . or else!

Panicked and alone, the steward tries to find the old witch once more. He travels on the backward lanes and wayward roads. That is, the road behind the road, the track beneath the track—that which is not seen but felt—and sure enough, that is exactly where he finds her. "Oh, Grandmother Baba, help me so! The sharpshooter has survived with deer in tow, and now the king is mad—what should I do?"

And in turn she responds:

"Well, then! We will have to give them a more difficult problem so that they will not solve it so quickly. Tell the king to send the sharpshooter to go to the land of 'I know not where' and bring back 'I know not what.' That is in truth the edge of destruction, where Shmat-Razum lives. Your sharpshooter will not complete this task in all eternity. He will either fail or get lost, and so your problem will be solved."

He pays her gold and then goes on his way to tell the king, who is now very pleased with this impossible task. Fedot, our dear sharpshooter, is informed of what he has no choice but to do. In despair he goes to his wife and tells her what is happening. She says, "Fear not, my dear husband. Go to sleep, as one always awakens wiser than before the dark."

Once more, she returns to her magic book, but this time the two youths cannot help her, as they do not know where or how to bring back Shmat-Razum, who lives at the edge of destruction. An impossible task, they tell her, which will take her husband at least 18 years to complete.

Now, Blue Dove, daughter of a royal king, wakes up her husband and tells him to go to the king and ask for the road's golden treasure—that is, the money for the trip. But before he leaves, she gives him two gifts: One is a ball, and the other is a piece of cloth.

With these two gifts, she offers instructions: "No matter where you find yourself, throw the ball before you, and wherever it rolls, do follow. As for the piece of cloth, whenever you are finished washing or eating, wipe your face with it. Both gifts are of my own making."

Her husband is grateful but equally afraid as he sets off on a treacherous path to the edge of destruction.

The king, now happy that Fedot is finally out of the picture, sends for his wife. Blue Dove goes with the royal command, and the king demands that she become his wife. "If you do not willingly become mine, I will take you by force." To which Blue Dove responds by laughing as she strikes the floor and once more becomes a bird, who simply flies out the window.

Yet Fedot is still on a treacherous path, as he is still searching daily for Shmat-Razum at the edge of destruction. Many moons go by when one day he stumbles upon a witch's hut. Baba Yaga invites him in and lets him rest his weary bones and heart. "There, there, my dear—have something to eat." Tired and alone, he eats what is offered, and then, as always, he cleans his face with his wife's cloth.

Baba Yaga awakens, her eyes now alert. "Where did you find this woven cloth? *It is my sister's!*"

And so Fedot tells her his tale, and in turn she decides to help him on his quest. Now with the full force of her magic, she summons all the animals in the entire land. "Do any of you know where Shmat-Razum can be found?" Yet no one knows. So, she goes to her magic book, and in an instant, two giants appear. "What dost thou need, dear?"

"My faithful helpers, take this traveler and me to the ocean and stop just in the middle above the very abyss."

Immediately the two giants seize the old woman and the sharpshooter. Like tall pillars, they hold them over the middle of the sea, where she asks all the water creatures: "Know any of you where Shmat-Razum is and how to find him?"

Yet no one knows.

Just as they are beginning to lose hope, an old frog suddenly appears from the depths of the watery abyss. *"Kwa-kwa*—I know where to find such a wonder, but I am far too old to leap there."

Baba Yaga responds, "Fear not, Fedot. Take this glass of milk and place this frog within it—carry her to where she tells you to go." He does as he is told, and the frog takes him to the edge of a river. It is there where she tells him to jump on her back. Fedot doubts himself for a moment, as she is a small frog, so frail in nature. How will she ever carry him? Yet, he does what he is told, and she begins to grow and grow. Together they cross the wide and vast river.

On the other side, she says, "At this river's edge lies a mountain, which you can see, yet inside it you will find a cave, and in that place, you will find Shmat-Razum."

Delighted that his search is almost over, Fedot enters the cave and quiets down. It is there where he finds Shmat-Razum, a genie of sorts who can materialize whatever is requested of him from the ether. Shmat-Razum is serving two old men, who are barking commands at him. "Make wine and bring forth a feast." The two old men continue to demand more and more things, and when they are filled to the brim, they leave the cave.

It is then when Fedot approaches Shmat-Razum and asks him to come and share a meal with him. The genie is so pleased to join Fedot because in the 30 years that he has served the old men, not once had they invited him to eat at their table! As a result, Shmat-Razum chooses to leave with Fedot.

Together they then journey home—a full tale that must be condensed here for our needs, so for brevity let me simply state that they travel the wide-open seas and return to the witch. They give her and the old frog gifts of thanks. They experience many challenges on the waters of the unknown, and then one day they finally return to Fedot's homeland. Once there, Blue Dove returns to meet her husband. The king hears of these things and wages a war against them. A battle ensues, but with the help of Shmat-Razum, the old king is defeated. Fedot and Blue Dove are then crowned king and queen. Healthy, wealthy, and wise, the entire kingdom flourishes in great harmony and happiness. And just like that, this ancient tale is now complete.

CHAPTER 5

AN ANCIENT LANGUAGE IS EVOKED

The most ancient language in the world is symbolic. It is woven by the psyche and made into matter through dreams and stories. Through this very story, we learn all about this ancient language that spins the mystical into the material; doing so shows us how to access both our Medial and Wild natures. We embark on a mythic quest to discover wholeness and balance where many different aspects of Self and society come into view. Let us now unpack this tale so that you can discover both the Medial and the Wild within you.

Our story begins with Fedot in the woods when he comes across a magnificent bird—a blue dove.[1] We learn here that perhaps we are all just like Fedot. That is because in the surprising moment of fully coming into contact with our own soulful and Medial essence, we may notice and marvel in its beauty, but we still do not recognize it for exactly what it is. We fail to see the numen of the Soul *because we have been conditioned to shoot it down.* So, both our story and healing begin here with a half-dead blue bird, an injured Medial Nature that has been pierced by the sharpshooter of either the self or the society, or both at the same time.

Now, if I asked you if you'd ever shoot down your own connection to your Soul, I imagine that you'd say no, but we see it so clearly in the eyes of so many that the Medial connection has been severely severed. I see this very often when I tell people what I do and then I hear why intuition is rubbish or dreams are meaningless. And then in the same breath the very same people will give me examples of times when they did have intuitive hits that turned out later to be true. Or when they had an experience that really shook them awake like seeing a deceased loved one—only to then dismiss their own experiences once again.

It is a vicious cycle of choosing not to see that injures the Medial Nature. It's a type of inner schism that tears one apart because no one can live authentically in this manner. It's too hard to walk topside through life like a little injured bird who has Medial gifts beyond measure but who chooses not to use them. And so, we see the half-alive Medial Nature pleading "Please don't kill me" both to the sharpshooters of the mind and society.

You must rescue the Medial Nature from your own harmful shots masked as self-doubt or inner criticism. If you have a gut instinct and you ignore it, you are shooting down your own Soul's guidance and insights. We must also save the Medial gifts from our culture's own cutting nature, which dismisses anything unknown, extraordinary, intuitive, and nonlinear. In our story, Blue Dove is the Medial connector to the Soul. She represents our connection to the unseen, where she can traverse back and forth like the great migrator that she is. She is the mediator as well as the mediumistic and oracular function within the psyche. She is the connector between the unseen and seen worlds. It is no accident that she is a dove in this story; her symbolic representation is vast and significant—just as you are. (In some alchemical texts the dove symbolically represents a person's soul after the unity of opposites has occurred.)

Our fairy tale then progresses, and we see that she tells the sharpshooter to take her home and then to strike her when she is sleeping. How bizarre. Yet this is actually not so strange if we dig a little deeper and look with Soul sight . . . The interior instruction is very clear: When I am asleep, hit me with the back of your right hand—which he does. Remember, at this point, Fedot and the blue bird are out of the enchantment of the woods. He has taken her back to his home, and this is when a striking breakthrough happens. That is when the Ego Self comes into direct and conscious contact with the Soul Self through that backhanded hit. In other words: The Medial Nature has been discovered through a surprising strike of consciousness.

To clarify, the Ego Self is the part of you that identifies as "you." It is the inner part of all of us that helps us to define where we begin and end. This is not the same thing as being egoic or having a monkey mind that is always thinking excessively. I mean the Ego Self here in the most classical sense of the term, in that it is the part of us that helps us to perceive the world in a healthy way. Good boundaries, for example, are activated through a healthy Ego Self. On the other hand, the Soul Self is just that—the Soul version of you. Both distinct parts of Self are brought together in this story through a breakthrough.

By Fedot *consciously* striking the blue bird, a connection is established between the ego and the Soul, and as a result the Soul-maiden is born. The injured blue bird is transformed from a half-alive Medial instinct into a Soul-maiden, or a Medial Maiden, our Blue Dove.

The word *maiden* here has nothing to do with age; it is simply a signifier of the level of trust that one has in their own connection to their soulful nature. A person can be a Medial maiden in their 70s if they have not consciously developed their Instinctual nature. This is also why you are here, reading these very words and mapping out the woods of your own psyche in order to develop and strengthen your own Instinctual nature—no matter your age or level of mastery.

When you make conscious contact with your soul, a breakthrough is almost always guaranteed because the instinctive nature is then consciously activated. The word *maiden* also shows us that an inner union or marriage has not yet occurred between the Soul Self and the Ego Self. That only happens later when Fedot and Blue Dove marry and when she says to him, "You knew how to get me. *Now learn how to live with me.*"

In other words, the story says, "Walk through life with me hand in hand *as partners*. Don't just find me in the enchanted woods as a half-aware, half-awake hunter of Spirit." This is the same thing as going on a meditation retreat, and then, as you drive home, you begin to forget all about your mindfulness practices, quickly picking up an old identity with all its habitual patterns. This story tells us to be conscious in Spirit—and in heart—throughout our lives. Use your Soul to guide you daily. Use your Medial and Wild nature in connection with your Ego Self while you are out grocery shopping and equally when you are out contemplating in the forest too.

If you have been denying your instincts for most of your life, it may very well feel like a strike of awakening to allow the Soul back in—to let it lead you forward. In many ways there is nothing else to do but to let yourself be struck. Let us once again not be fooled; a strike can sometimes hit like a bolt of lightning, which can cause discomfort. Otherwise, we would have been told, "Oh, lovely sharpshooter, take this feather and smudge me awake."

This is not so. She says, "Whack me with the back of your hand." In other words—wake up! The sharpshooter thinks he is hitting her, but in reality, he is really striking himself awake. In other words, conscious awareness is beginning to be cultivated at this point. In the story, the blue bird hits the floor and then unveils herself as a magnificent woman. In parallel, sometimes when we hit rock bottom, it is then when we have the greatest opportunity for real and meaningful transformation, because the Soul has the opportunity to make itself heard. Rock bottom often strips away the noise where one can do nothing else but listen as the Soul unfurls its beauty into full view. It is often in crisis when we come to discover our own Medial Natures.

I have had many experiences in my life where I have allowed sleep to cover my eyes by choosing to see the mundane over the mystical for ease of fitting in, or when I simply made bad choices *when I knew better*. I have done this far more than I care to recount, but I will say this: A move away from the numinous can happen so easily. Like when you know you should leave a relationship, but you choose to stay in it while it limps along, and both of you become numb automatons, sitting in front of the TV. Or when you choose to get "lost" when you actually know which direction to take but are afraid of the enormity of the leap and what it will require of you. So, you simply coast along in the land of lost Souls. It can also happen when you are hiding in fear of truly being seen.

Soul work is not always easy or comfortable, but it is highly rewarding and freeing. And through this story, we learn how to overcome these obstacles by consciously calling the Soul back to us. Yet, in order to do this, we must see life through our oracle eyes. That is, you must set your sight so close to the earth that your cells remember that you are made from the land. You must also lift your sight to the sky so that you remember that you are from the constellations. Both sand and star are within you, and when you remember that, you are ready to walk once more as a living, breathing creature both Medial and Wild.

This in essence is the true test of the "maiden" passage in relation to the Medial initiation. Can you stay awake and stand true even when those around you wish to control you or cut you down? Can you keep contact with that which is precious even when those around you cannot (or choose not to) see with the eyes of the Soul? Can you choose the path of the Medial who lives in both worlds? That is, the world of here and the world of there: Soul and earth, Spirit and matter, head and heart. Can you choose to stay awake in both realms even when life is not easy? Equally, can you choose to stay awake even when life is a breeze? Sometimes the latter is even harder because comfort can be an absolute awareness killer.

In story and as in life, a maiden is often not one who is in her full expression of power as a crone or queen would be. But she is still magnificent *because* she is Medial and because of this her intuitive and soulful gifts are apparent. In many ways, it is like thinking that because you meditated for five minutes that that makes you a master—sadly not. No matter where we find ourselves, time, effort, maintenance, and connection are required for the Instinctual and Medial self to not only survive but thrive. We see this so clearly as our story and lives develop, as there is always something new to learn.

THE CONNECTING OF THE EGO SELF AND THE MEDIAL WOMAN

Fedot and Blue Dove are married at this point. In other words, the Ego Self and the Soul Self are joined—they are consciously connected to each other through the Medial Nature, but it's early days. This is like the beginning of a Spiritual practice where it all feels so exciting and awe-inspiring. *However, the real practice starts when the excitement ends.* When you consciously show up daily, even when you don't feel like it, or when it would be easier and more convenient not to. As you commit to working hand in hand with the unseen, you will notice that life changes miraculously, but this isn't to say that it will be locked into a particular feeling state—look at our Fedot. *His quest takes years, and he goes through many emotions.* Life in itself is a quest, and this story shows us that it is how we show up that makes all the difference.

As the time passes, Blue Dove notices her husband working so very hard. This symbolically speaks to something almost all of us have to contend with: the need for the Ego Self to work hard in order to receive "rewards" or "sustenance." This work can be focused either externally, like through a job in the outside world, or, in psyche speak, the work here can represent the internal job of filtering all the information the Ego receives, as well as keeping the tyrannical king within happy, who demands "things." (The king's demands are often hypercritical and strive for a level of perfection that is impossible to meet. It is a never-ending list of needing to reach an ideal of whatever sort, like appearance/money/status, etc.)

The king symbolically represents power, authority, and rules as well as any overinflated, self-enforced, and egoic internalized demands. Now, Fedot is the king's hunter—that is his job, and he must hunt in order to survive. In many ways the Ego Self has a hard lot in life. It is there to keep us in order, to help us see this world of reality in its concreteness and without its faculties we would suffer. It is also there to help us survive in a very real world of money, power, boundaries, and structures. It is there to help us in the realm of the mundane day-to-day, and without its beneficial perception, we could slip into the ether and lose ourselves altogether.

Without an Ego Self it would be like having no boundaries and only seeing the color purple everywhere. And then all of a sudden someone gives you glasses (Ego Sight), and looking through the lenses, you see that the shades of purple were actually flowers—irises. And then with your Soul Self, you remember that Iris is a Medial maker, a Soulful flower herself. In other words, you must see with both sets of sight as each are helpful and necessary. You can drown in the collective unconscious if you are not careful. We need both a healthy Ego Self and Soul Self to navigate life in a balanced and well-integrated manner. Consensual reality and the mystical unconscious require strong conscious awareness—*your* strong awareness of where you begin and end in relation to everything else around you, both unseen and seen.

Let's return to our story of Fedot and Blue Dove—we know that he is a hunter for the king and that he works very hard as a sharpshooter. In fact, after some time, Blue Dove feels very sorry for him because he is enduring such difficult labor. So she says to him, "Go and borrow some money and buy some silk." Now, he is a hunter. What exactly is he going to do with the silk? He has no idea, but he goes and buys the silk anyway. This is similar to receiving a Soulful insight that tells you to move somewhere or start something that is entirely new to you and then having no idea what to do after. We are required to trust in the first step without often having further information.

At this point, we could say that Fedot has the good sense to listen to divine or Soulful inspiration, and at the same time he is also developing good Ego Strength in the journey of *doing and becoming*. Let me quickly clarify here what I mean by "Ego Strength." I mean it again in the psychological sense of the word and not the common use of the word *ego*. Ego Strength is not the same thing as the egoic monkey mind that sprouts thoughts incessantly or the part of self that thinks that it is better than everyone else. Ego Strength is the part of you that knows how to tolerate frustration and stress. It is the part of you that allows for delayed gratification. It is also the part of you that helps curb selfish behaviors and heal emotional patterns before they become ingrained as unhelpful and rigid ways of living. Parents become well acquainted with Ego Strength when they begin to teach (and mirror) these very things to their children.

For Fedot, Ego Strength is in part that he goes to the market and buys the silk (he listens to the Soul), but he has no idea what the rewards, if any, will be at this point. Yet he shows up, and in doing so, he tolerates the discomfort of stepping into the unknown. It is his Ego Strength that helps him to move forward under the guidance of the Soul. As it is your own Ego Strength that will help you during any times of change under the guidance of your own Soul.

In order to move past a certain patterned way of being and living, one must do something differently for change to be evoked. The old inner and outer structures must give way so that growth can occur. Perhaps you've heard of the businesswoman Sara Blakely, who started the empire that is Spanx. Before she started her company, she was selling fax machines door-to-door, and in a bolt of insight, a thought occurred to her: *This can't be my life—I'm in the wrong story.* That insight could have overwhelmed her into self-pity or inaction, but instead she chose to focus her attention on the unknown. Fast-forward some time when she was getting ready for an event and realized that she didn't have the right undergarments to provide a seamless look under white pants. So, she cut the feet off her control-top pantyhose, and the idea for Spanx was seeded. Later, when she was wondering if her idea was good enough to actually become a business, she randomly turned on the TV to an episode of *Oprah*, only to see her talking about how she cut off her pantyhose. In that moment, she knew she was on to something! Synchronicity confirming Soul-led inspiration and action.

That said, though, Soulful insight doesn't mean the work is done. In fact, many times it means that the work is just beginning, but the journey hits differently. The journey feels better, more honest, and more often than not it is also more rewarding. Anyone who has ever written a book will know what I mean—there are times when you feel like giving up, when you think no one will read it, if there is even a point, and yet a writer shows up and writes regardless of all these things. Discomfort of the unknown must be tolerated on the path toward becoming who you want to be. You have to ask: *Who do I need to become in order to live the life I want to live?*

If you have something you'd like to do or be, you must step in its direction, you must take action (it can be a small step—just start), even if you don't know what all the steps are going to be. It is learning to walk your talk and stay the course even when you are in the dark while trusting that your Soul will illuminate the path forward, step by step. This is what it means to see in the dark, to shut down the thoughts of the critical and overanalytical mind in order to step into the liminal and Soulful place where possibilities are born. In this liminal place, you are in the darkness, as it is like gestating in a womb both fertile and dark, after which something new is birthed into the world.

It is the initiation between the Ego Self and the Soul Self that teaches us to walk our talk. It is here where we learn to find congruence between who we really are and who we say we are. It is also through this initiation where your destiny can be retrieved—where untold possibilities are present. In this place of possibilities stockings can turn into Spanx and fate can change into destiny. Familial karma can be released, and patterns can be broken if you allow yourself to take a quantum leap guided by the Medial Nature—where you close one chapter and open a new book altogether. These things are possible, but you must move forward into the unknown with your Soul sight switched on. And a small note here: This isn't the same thing as defiantly moving forward, sometimes waiting for Soulful inspiration or "the right idea" to strike is part of the initiation. You don't want to plough ahead without inspiration, as that is simply self-sabotage. That's the small mind convincing you that it knows better, but it is really only the Soul self that can see the larger picture.

So how do we tap into the larger picture? Our story has some guidance. At this point Fedot goes home and gives the silk to his wife. And then, like most of us would do when we first begin to listen to Soulful nudges, he panics. *What have I done?* And so, in return, his partner, the Medial Nature, tells him to go to sleep: "All things shall be wiser in the morning, my love."

Sleep is the mysterious portal that naturally instigates renewal and healing in both myth and life. If you recall, the blue bird asks Fedot to let her fall into slumber before he hits her. Here, too, we see that she tells him to go to sleep, and when he will awaken, he will be wiser than before. Falling asleep is the gateway into the dreaming world, and awakening from sleep is the doorway into the waking world. It is the portal that we all easily cross over into nightly, a threshold of reality that turns imaginal—and we do this without even blinking. It is so normal to fall asleep and dream, but where are we really when we are dreaming? For all intents and purposes, we are in the land of the Medial, the soulscape of that which is, a vortex of pure creation.

Equally, as we leave the dreaming world and reenter our consensual reality, we do this through the portal of awakening from sleep. Scientifically, these passageways of consciousness are known as the hypnagogic and hypnopompic states of sleep. They are scientific terms for liminal consciousness where your awareness has the capacity to be "awake" in both realms. Liminal passages are also the playground for the modern Medial Woman, as this is where magic often happens in both real life and in fairy tales.

Blue Dove, our Medial Maiden, goes and stands under the sky. It is beautiful, and she is at home and comfortable in the dark of the evening. It is then that she opens her magic book and calls forth Soul-guided solutions that will solve her problems in the realm of the material world. And so, we learn here that in this space we have access to Soulful and instinctive guidance. In other words, our Medial awareness is activated when the Ego Mind goes to sleep, and through this liminal passage of awakening, we can access highly valuable oracular guidance and solutions.

It's also interesting to note that in some versions of this fairy tale, Blue Dove does not have a magic book; rather, she is the one who summons her own magic. She stands in the dark of the night and two youths appear because she summons them. Perhaps the symbolic objects changed over time in fear that she might be too powerful. Isn't that an all-too-familiar statement for the archaic and wise feminine who is connected to her Medial Nature?

In this manner, it is the book that then does the magic, but not her. Imagine if she could summon intuitive and instinctive magic from within herself. Well, then, she would be quite a force to be reckoned with. Ultimately, this is something we all have to discover for ourselves—our inner abilities unaided by external things, the bedrock of who we really are. We may first discover our own Medial and instinctive gifts mirrored through words in a book, and then we must learn to call them forth without the book. Learning and then practicing as the great weaving and reweaving of all things.

So there she is, our magic instigator, Blue Dove, who opens her book, and then suddenly two youths appear, and she says to them:

"Take this silk and wield it so. Make it that it may become the most beautiful tapestry in all the land. Let all the images of the king's domain be set upon it, and do this within the hour."

Here we see the pure potential and potency of what it means to uncover our Instinctual gifts and Soulful talents through the medium of the Medial Nature. The unleashing of both the creative and resourceful aspects of self—the parts within that are one with the muse and that can act as open channels for divine inspiration. Blue Dove is also very clear in adding the king's images onto the tapestry. Like any good oracle, she can see the future unfolding from her higher perspective. She requests the creation of this tapestry knowing that the king will see value in it because he will see his kingdom in it. In other words, she knows how to use the tyrannical mind, or the tyrannical society to her benefit by maneuvering appropriately through relying on her Spiritual sight.

Adaptability is a highly effective skill set that can be remarkable when necessary. For example, if you have set intentions for your life and you would like to see a specific outcome, the Soul self, the Instinctual self, may ask you to bend or move (to adapt) in a way that you may not be able to fully understand or be comfortable with. This is so that you can actually move out of any comfort zone (or any uncomfortable societal structure) and into a better way of living. It may also simply be because your Soul sight can see things you cannot, so trust and adaptability are required in order to move forward positively.

In our story, Fedot's (the Ego Self's) comfort zone is that he is a hunter and that he works very hard for the king. Here we see that the intent of the Ego Self at this stage is in line with the will of the king. *Yet, we do not want our intent of will (our hunt) to be aligned with a tyrannical structure that is either internal or external.* So, we must pay attention to when our Ego Self is not in line with the will of the Soul Self and when there is an imbalance of intention. The Soul Self nudges Fedot and in essence says, "There is another way." Eventually, from following Soulful steps, our hunter Fedot becomes king, but it all starts with that first step of buying the silk, one small Soulful step in the mysteriously right direction relying on the skill set of adaptability.

Eventually, the hunter of the mind, the inner intent and will of the Ego Self, becomes aligned with the will of the Soul. This is when true alchemy begins to occur because both aspects of Self are in alignment and with that one stands in their true and balanced strength. So even though Fedot (the Ego Self) is afraid and panicked, Blue Dove (the Medial connection to the Soul Self) is calm and secure knowing that the Soulful creation, the tapestry, holds immense value.

THE CREATIVE SELF AND A NOTE ON WORTHINESS

Fedot wakes up to find the tapestry and is then instructed by the Medial Self to go to the market and sell it—but not to put a price on it. At the market, the tapestry is bought by the king's steward for 10 thousand rubles after a lively debate among everyone present. Medial gifts are Soul woven as they are gifted from the ether, and because of this they are intrinsically special. As such, Soul creations are always beyond mundane measure, and this is why Blue Dove instructs him not to assign a price.

If you create something that stems from the Medial Nature, don't place its real value on a price, because you already know its worth. It is beyond price—it is priceless.

Perhaps Fedot would have asked for one thousand rubles—thinking that this was a fair price for labor and the cost of the tapestry. Yet they see it, the light woven onto the tapestry—the images of the king's entire domain—and they pay Fedot far more than he would have guessed. In essence, if you create something that is truly gifted from the Medial Nature, know that its value is intrinsic, and then if you get a price for it in the marketplace, great, but either way, its worth is still immense, regardless of whether other people can recognize it. The main question here is, can you recognize the immense value of your own luminosity? Blue Dove knew the tapestry's value the moment she beckoned for it to be made, and so Fedot (the Ego Self) gets far more than he even bargained for as a result of listening to Blue Dove's Medial guidance.

We must create our Soul creations in their entirety for that purpose. If others see a value to it, wonderful, and if not, it does not matter. They are beyond this world, brought through you *for you*. So many people lose sight of creating because they don't think their creations can make them money (maybe that's true, and maybe it isn't), but one must also create for the sake of creating itself because this is how we keep the Medial Nature alive and well—we tend to the psychic waters from which true creativity comes. In relation to this, I hear Bukowski somewhat barking that no matter what circumstances you find yourself in, you have got to create—whether you're in a coal mine or a room with three kids.

In university, I had a friend whose parents barely escaped from former Yugoslavia during the war. Before they fled, they were both licensed lawyers. Lo and behold, life happened, and her father became a taxi driver to keep his family financially afloat while her mother worked in a laundromat. And in that time-space, her mother sat in that sweaty, hot, and unbearably noisy place and she created. She put pen to paper and fiercely channeled innovation in that space. There was no right light or space other than those she was creating from within. The Medial power is immense; it can and will save a life if one can move beyond needing "conditions" to be just right. And the Soul will always find a way to flourish—as did they.

So, if you find yourself in better circumstances but with a demented cat crawling up your back, perhaps that is actually your Wild and Medial Nature clawing you awake, saying, *Go out and create!* Unleash yourself from the cage of "what if" and "what will be," and please do not wait for perfect conditions, as they are few and far between. You will know what to do because the instruction will come from within you and following it will make you feel vitally alive. And remember, creating isn't just about making things or artistic endeavors; it is about sculpting a life and developing relationships that help you to feel both secure and free—*at the same time.*

Ultimately, the Medial maiden becomes a Medial Woman when she unleashes her instinctive gifts, when she shines so brightly and creates so Soulfully that she does exactly what she came here to do: to love so deeply and to live so widely that life itself expands because of her. In fact, don't our times call for this very thing? Isn't it time for us all to unbind that which is life-giving? The Medial initiation will ask you to step into your life so that you don't just use your magic, but you become it instead. If you choose to embark on this journey, you will then be able to stand alone in the middle of the night, the glorious unknown, and truly unleash it all, completely unafraid of your inner power as a Medial Woman, one in her own.

THE COVETING OF THE MEDIAL NATURE AND THE NEED FOR WILD DISCERNMENT

In our tale we are told over and over again that it is Blue Dove's extraordinary beauty that drives both the king and steward crazy. They seek to own her, control her, express dominion over her. The Soul Self, when truly shown, is so beautiful that people often covet it when they are disconnected from their own true natures.

Sometimes, when you stand in your Soul-centered power, there will be those who will seek to knock you down or control you. They will wonder how you do what you do, or they may even mimic you and claim aspects of you (or your creations) as their own. They are attracted to your Soul-shine because they can't remember how to find their own. In times like this, it becomes even more important to shine brightly while compassionately showing others how to find their own Soulful centers. Boundaries and empathy make a good pair on the path toward wholeness, wellness, and empowerment.

By now you also know that this mythic journey is one that happens both within you and in the world outside of you too. We see this clearly through the king and the steward in this story as they represent both *internal and external structures* that need adjusting, depending on what is happening both in your own life and in this fairy tale.

Perhaps it's people in the outside world that try and knock you off course, or maybe it is something within you that tries to do the same thing, like starting a project but never finishing it because of an internalized fear of success/failure or harsh inner criticism. Or, alternatively, having a critical "whoever" who doesn't support your goals, so you never start in the first place. These are just some ways that our Soulful natures can become restricted, and we are the only ones who can release ourselves from constriction—permission must be granted from you *for you*.

In this story, the king commands the steward to get rid of the husband, Fedot. The Ego Self is to be killed. This can be read in many ways, like needing to allow an old identity to die so that the authentic self can then lead. We will tackle this concept of Ego Death more acutely in Chapter 6. For now, we return to the steward who is our trickster/fool in the story and without whom our story would not actually progress, and as a result, we would not experience greater growth or integration. He does one thing thinking it will result in a specific action, but then something else entirely happens. How many times has that happened to you? Some of the best and most uncomfortable adventures of my life started because I naively did not know better, just like our steward in the story who represents both a certain lack of awareness, hopeful optimism, and desperation all at the same time.

Conversely, the king here at this point is still the superpower of the mind—he is the loud and dominant motivator or force of behavior. At this stage in our journey, he also represents any beliefs and behaviors that are unconscious in nature, meaning any underlying internal impulses that influence your actions that you are not consciously aware of that keep you stuck in a holding pattern. The king's dominating power is needing an overhaul, as are any unconscious or limiting beliefs that are getting in the way of your growth and happiness.

Whatever is submerged in consciousness requires the higher aspects of self to send a wake-up call in order to shift awareness so that wholeness and well-being can be nurtured once again.

In our story the wake-up call begins to kick in when the steward is steeped in grief and panic after the king orders him to get rid of Fedot—otherwise his own life is at risk. So, he walks and walks as he tries to hatch a plan, and somehow he finds himself on backward roads and in wasted places when he comes upon a stranger—a Wild Witch, Baba Yaga. Here we find that even so-called foolish and crooked paths can lead us to the Wild Nature within.

What an absolute blessing disguised as an ugly old woman.

Sometimes the things that seem most corrupt, the ones most twisted to look at are those who have learned to adapt best, hidden in plain sight for those brave enough to venture into the deep dark woods. The land is backward, and the place is wasted because *she*, the Wild Woman, our earthen mother, has been relegated to the edges. Perhaps then only a "fool" can venture far enough into the Wild out of sheer necessity when the rest of society is sitting in the comfort of delusion, demanding that there is no need to go within, saying that it is too dark, too inconvenient, too much to handle, *too Wild*. In that case, may we all experience the leap of a fool that is so naive in nature that it stumbles forward without realizing that it is helping to rejoin the center to its Wild edges.

CHAPTER 6

THE BABA YAGA EFFECT

Baba Yaga symbolically represents both the Wild Nature and our Wild Woman. She is seen as a witch in this fairy tale.[1] And in many other stories, she is described as a vile and twisted old hag—scary down to the very bones that she boils. Traditionally, her house stands on two chicken legs and twirls around like a cauldron made straight from hell. She is either good or bad, depending on who is telling the story, and as I am the storyteller here, I will say this—she can pour either honey or salt, depending on what you need, like a good grandmother who has seen too much and knows exactly when to lovingly call you out on your bullshit. She can *and will* morph into a fierce creature as required in order to scare a person or society out of complacency.

Sadly, Baba Yaga is also framed as a witch because that is how our connection to the Wild Nature was squashed into submission over time by large and dominant societal forces. She went from being a revered Wild Woman to a Wild Witch and then an old evil hag, as that which is other is that "witch" is scary. And history has shown us what happens to witches: They are drowned, burned alive, and strung up by their so-called neighbors and friends. Here we see a great fear brewing both internally and externally—a fear that will remain until every woman and Wild thing is free. The fear reads like this:

Don't go out into the woods because a Wild Witch lives there, and she will catch you (or worse, your innocent children!), make mincemeat of you, and then grind your bones into dust.

In other words, both the Wilderness and the Wild Woman/Witch are to be feared as death is the impending result of contact with either. This narrative is also how we bind our children because we teach them what to fear—we condition their perspectives before they even get started.

Additionally, we are taught to fear the witch within because if she is "seen" by those outside her, those who fear her power, she will be strung up and made into an example, particularly in times of chaos, when the collective craves a scapegoat.

Once again, the fear reads like this: The Wild Woman/Witch within is so powerful that if those around you even glimpse her in you, it may result in death. You may be outed by your neighbors who fear your Soul sight or your ability to heal and alter reality.

Both fears result in death. In one scenario, we die at the hands of the witch in the wilderness, and in the other we die at the hands of society. We are damned either way if we don't clear the lens through which we see the Wild both within ourselves and in the world at large.

Now, I know this sentiment of fear may sound a bit extreme, and we don't want to linger in fear-based thinking for very long. But for our purposes, it is very helpful to shed light on how these internalized fears can present themselves and in turn what we can do about them. Even in very tolerant and open-minded places, discomfort with both the Wild and Medial Nature *still occurs*. Equally, tolerance and celebration of the Medial Nature online is not the same thing as tolerance of it on the ground. Recently, I had an experience that reminded me of how implicit internalized fear can be in relation to this.

I went to my local printing shop, where I am somewhat of a regular, and in that bustling space of people sending packages and printing pages, it was business as usual. The employee, who recognized me, nodded a friendly greeting and then opened the document that I needed to print. The document was titled *Sisterhood of the Seers*, which is the name of my 44-card oracle deck. The teller's mood changed so sharply when she read the word *seer*. She wasn't rude or mean; she was just visibly uncomfortable.

"Ah, ma'am, is *this* the correct document, the one titled [whispers] *Seers*?"

Yes, this is how pervasive fear and societal frowning can be that even printing a page with a "loaded" word can create palpable fear and discomfort. Ultimately, it stems from the discomfort of the Wild and Medial Natures within us all. Perhaps she read the word *seer* and feared what it mirrored for her or what the other customers would say. It can be hard to see an aspect of yourself printed in black-and-white or recognize fear reflected in the faces of those around you. What is a seer, after all, other than someone who can see with their second sight? A Medial, who is comfortable with the Wild unknown, just like our very own Blue Dove.

Ultimately, if just the utterance of the word made the teller's hairs stand up on the back of her neck, then imagine releasing not just the words but the actual Wild/Medial Woman herself. This challenge is at the bedrock of our intrapsychic task and Medial initiation. Perhaps this is also why the journey is mythic in nature, as you must call the Wild and Medial back to you from both the far edges of the world as well as from the disowned places within.

Relegated by the cages of hyper-rationalism, we have locked in our sisters both Medial and Wild out of conditioned fear. And we are tasked to release them both within us and out in the world at large. Luckily for us, it is easy to step out of fear and to clear the lens of perception—we simply need to look again to see things anew and from a higher perspective instead of believing either the implicit or explicit fear that maintains that the wilderness and the Wild woman are to be feared as death may be the impending result of contact with either. We come to learn that we are actually brought closer to that which is life-giving when we come into contact with our Wild and Medial Natures. When we allow the Wild and Medial to be seen, to come out and play, well-being naturally returns. So, if you catch a glimpse of her in the mirror, greet her with a warm welcome.

Here is a new way of seeing this entire matter:

Go out into the Wild and collect your bones from the One Who Knows:[2] *our Old Wolf the Medial Seer . . . as she has kept them safe for you.*

Through reclaiming your Wild knowing and Medial sight, you will then be shown how to live and dream harmoniously with all that is. If you don't know how to do this, don't be discouraged, as you intrinsically have access to your Medial Nature, and because of this, you can retrieve the information that you need. A simple but effective way of realizing this is by requesting helpful guidance to come to you through meditation or in your nighttime dreams.

Ultimately, we lose our connection to the Wild Woman through fear and conditioning, but we can reclaim it through higher awareness, heart-courage, and Soul-sight, which are all aspects of the Medial Nature. Through a Medial way of seeing, we can perceive both our inner and outer worlds in a way that bring us harmony, peace, and well-being. We must also use our Medial ways of seeing and sensing to help the Wild Nature outside of us. Remember that this is a bidirectional union, one that requires your presence and active participation in both the realms of your inner world and objective reality.

Our time calls for Medial Women to rise up in service to the Wild Nature that exists both within us and outside in the world around us. The Medial instinct must return en masse so that we can help all life, and this in return will help us all, for the issue is simple: Without us, Wild Woman dies. "Without Wild Woman, we die. Para Vida, for true life, both must live."[3]

In order to understand the importance and multiple layers between the Medial and the Wild and the many ways that it can play out, I would like to share a story with you of a black leopard who came to live in an eco-sanctuary called Jukani, which is located in South Africa. This story is from a documentary called *The Animal Communicator*, and it is well worth watching if you get an opportunity to, as the narrative shows how our link to the Wild Nature is not just an interior psychological connection but also a connection that can be used in the outer world.[4]

Leopards are magnificent beings—they are strong, sleek, and instinctually stealthy. I am always humbled by their presence, so I find it hard to think about the fact that this poor animal spent the majority of his life in the harshest of conditions. Constrained in a zoo and bound to a small enclosure, living a life of misery like so many other animals are currently experiencing right now. In a stroke of luck, he was finally released from the zoo and sent to Jukani. Once transferred, everyone anticipated that this leopard, now called Diablo, would want to explore the vast natural environment available to him. Yet he still refused to come out of his night shelter. He would aggressively growl at anyone who would come close to him, and this unhappy situation carried on for about six months.

The owners of the sanctuary, Jurgen and Karen, really didn't know what to do, as the situation was becoming dire and all methods of helping him were not working. They were really worried about losing him, and they didn't want that to be the case. Sadly, most big cats who cannot be rehabilitated are often sent to canned hunting sites where they meet an inevitable and painful death. When I watched this story, my heart really opened up for Jurgen (a cop turned conservationist) because it was clear that he just wanted what was best for this leopard. As a result, they agreed to have a woman come to *speak with* the leopard because they felt desperate. A woman who describes herself as a professional interspecies communicator.

A woman whom I would call a Wild Medial.

In the documentary, Jurgen stated that he was highly skeptical of anyone who claimed that they could telepathically communicate with animals. I think this is a fair enough statement for most people. Yet it was one that was about to be turned upside down. The animal communicator, Anna, was given no prior information before arriving at the site. The meeting was also recorded via the documentary and has many other witnesses to confirm what happened. On the day, she simply went and sat near to where the leopard, Diablo, was. In the documentary there is a stillness between the two of them. Neither leopard nor woman are moving. She was in fact able to communicate with him through nonverbal communication—what I would call psychic or Medial communication.

Through their interaction, she learned that he didn't like the name Diablo because of the negative associations connected to it. He also wanted to know what happened to two other leopards that lived in the zoo with him prior to his move to Jukani. Anna listened, and then she communicated back to him. She told him that she would ask about the leopards, and then she reassured him that these humans would not demand or request anything of him. She told him that he was truly safe and secure in this new space. She then also relayed this information to every other human who was there.

There is a moment in the documentary where you can see skepticism turn into awe, where conditioned beliefs are dropped and replaced with reverence. In that moment I found it hard not to tear up. Imagine if all of us could acknowledge that we really are in connection to everything around us, that nature is actually in communion *with us*, and we are simply not awakened enough to listen—or so few of us are.

That very same afternoon, Diablo came out of his shelter and explored the lay of the land. Months and months of difficulty were resolved via one Medial conversation. Later in the documentary, Jurgen goes to the leopard and speaks *with him*—not at him. He tells him that he thinks he is the most beautiful being, thanks him for being there, and then shares information as to what happened to the two other leopards that were at the zoo. Jurgen also tells him once again that they would never demand anything of him in this space—in this sanctuary.

With wisdom, he then changes his name to Spirit.

There is a moment in the documentary when this tough ex-cop with a heart of gold cries when he realizes what has actually happened. That nature has spoken. That Spirit can speak. That Wild living, breathing things are able to communicate with us not just through body language but via something larger—our Medial Natures. I imagine what that depth of discovery must have felt like for Jurgen in that very moment—perhaps instant and indescribable—to move from disbelief to embodied knowing. I wish the same for you, especially if you find yourself steeped in doubt.

Later, in a wonderful turn of events, the two leopards that were left at the zoo were brought to live at Jukani. Spirit lived in peace and serenity surrounded by humans who loved him until he passed away. I shared this story with you in the hopes of showing you exactly how the Medial Nature is linked to both mother nature and the Wild Nature within. Your Medial Nature is the key to connecting to both Wild Woman within you and wild nature outside of you, as both psyche and physicality are linked.

In an interview, Anna shared how her ability to nonverbally communicate with animals was switched on. She was on a nature retreat with a guide who was teaching the group the art of tracking animals. One night, she had this moment where a bolt of insight came through where she saw three wolves near a river where they had killed an elk. The next morning, she told everyone what she had experienced. Later that same day, they hiked and discovered that exact scene as she had described. That waking vision helped her track both her Wild and Medial Nature. If you, too, go out into nature as a Medial, you may also hear both Wild Woman and the Wild speak.

In my 20s, I had a big dream about seven wolves who stood up on their hind legs to greet me. They were standing on the opposite side of a large pool and just watched me until I woke up. In the dream, I felt apprehension because I did not know what to do in response to them. I wanted to jump into the water to swim to them, but I held myself back out of a sense of not trusting my instinct enough. Yet, through that dream, I was able to find one of my spiritual teachers—a woman who was part of a sisterhood of dreamers. It really was the beginning of a calling that helped me reconnect to Spirit, intuition, and the Wild Instinct. I am happy to say that I have honored that call, and I hope you will too.

WHEN YOU BECOME A STRANGER TO YOURSELF, YOU ARE CLOSER THAN YOU THINK

Let us now return to the nature of our interior woods, where we once again meet with Blue Dove and Fedot. We turn inward so that we may uncover the next leg of the Medial Woman's mythic initiation and journey. *That is your journey.* As a quick refresher:

At this point in our mythic story, the steward has "accidentally" run into our Wild Baba Yaga, who tells him to make Fedot go on a journey to fetch the deer with the golden antlers. This is meant to be an impossible task, one completed at the outer reaches of the 13th kingdom, but Blue Dove summons her magic, and in an instant, the two youths appear with the deer in hand. Here we see that Medial gifts can solve impossible tasks in an instant, but why a deer specifically? As we know, no symbol is accidental in life, myth, or dreams.

Deer are both instinctual and gentle creatures by nature. They are also animals sacred to the ancient Wild Woman bloodline.[5] We see in our story that this is not just an average deer—it is one that has golden antlers. Gold in folktales often symbolizes the great treasure of the psyche and Spirit, alerting us to the inner riches that we are about to rediscover. This retrieval of the Instinctual Self, the golden deer, occurs in the outer reaches of the 13th land through the magical and mediumistic abilities of the Medial Nature. This is our psychic gold.

Why, then, the 13th kingdom?

In many systems of belief, the number 13 is considered unlucky or even dangerous. On the contrary, many feminists have argued that the number actually represents the divine feminine and as such has been intentionally shrouded in suppression and superstition over time. For me, the number is simply good because I was born on the 13th, yet when I reflect on this number in relation to our Wild and Medial story, it opens up an awareness of the link to the unseen realms through the medium of tarot.

In one sense, tarot can be looked at as an archetypal map of consciousness both personal and collective. A map of inner/outer rings of awareness in which we see that death has its place—its seat being the 13th number. And so just as a 13th day can mark a life, the very same number can celebrate death. In our heart of hearts, we also know that perhaps the fear of a number is likely because of a deeper fear of change, loss, and suffering—even death itself. The remedy, then, is often compassion as we meet endings and change with our hearts wide open, leaning in to an ancient knowing that teaches us how to move through these transitions with ease and grace.

During the very early stages of writing this book, I had the following dream, which helped me understand this matter more deeply.

In the dream, I find myself standing in a bookstore. The shelves hold hundreds of old books, as well as new, shiny ones.

I pick up a book and leaf through its pages, noticing beautiful images of landscapes. I then stop on one particular book and open it up, only to find that it is written in a foreign language. Strangely, I understand the words, but I cannot remember what the name of the language is. Then I notice a book titled *The Medial Woman*, with my name next to it. Of course, I open it up, only to discover that I'd actually written a book on death and grief.

I woke up startled.

It is natural to want to sit topside in the light, but it often takes the darkness to illuminate us. In this part of our Medial initiation, we must accept that it often takes an Ego Death or an identity death to transform ourselves, as all the familiar and comforting ways of being must be laid to rest. This includes ways of thinking and believing; one's identity, purpose, and even moral compass must undergo transformation. In many ways we all suffer endings throughout the course of our lives, but the Ego Death that occurs in relation to the Medial initiation is one that requires an emptying-out of sorts. We must empty ourselves of the notions that we hold on to too tightly in order to not just engage with the Medial Nature, but to become moved by it.

We must surrender both the conditioned ideas of the mind and the ingrained ways of behaving in order to allow higher consciousness to take the lead. In this journey we often also discover that we arrive at higher consciousness through disruption, and as many acute writers have previously noted, coming to consciousness is seldom a serene act. Yet, when we surrender to these required endings with grace, we come to discover that there is indeed an ancient language within us, one that can be understood without needing to be named, an archaic knowing that tells us that the Instinctual Nature is woven with equal doses of the Medial and Wild, as well as that of life and death. And that just as you honor life and grace, you must equally honor death and magic. Through this initiation, you will also come to intimately discover that there is a middle path, a delicate balance between will and surrender, and that you stand in the center of both. Medial women intrinsically know how to traverse between these thresholds skillfully and mindfully—the key, then, is consciously allowing this to happen, to move away from resisting any change and endings while gracefully traversing the in-between of what was and what shall be, to not only learn how to survive the liminal but to discover how to thrive in it too.

In our folktale we see that the changes that are occurring are happening because the king is forcing Fedot to go and retrieve a golden deer. This is extremely uncomfortable for Fedot, who has been forced to complete this strange task. At the same time, the king is pleased with the idea that Fedot will never be able to achieve this goal because it is indeed a challenging task. So here we see the symbolic confirmation of the necessity for change and death to first occur in order for transformation to happen. **The Ego Self must surrender to the will of the Instinctual Self. If this does not occur, then both the Wild and Medial Natures are stunted. No further growth can then occur, and as a result the individual becomes stuck.**

So, one must cross the threshold of initiation at this point, allowing the old ways of doing and being to be laid to rest. You will need *consciously* to choose to cross this threshold. It is also very normal for this stage of initiation to feel like a death, and it can be quite dramatic. But here's the silver lining: Our Medial Woman retrieves the deer *with ease*.

In other words, this doesn't necessarily need to be hard—it can be easy if you allow it to be.

Your Medial Nature can retrieve Instinctual insights with ease once your Ego Self gets out of the way. The Ego Self needs to become in service to the Instinctual/Soul Self and not the other way around. Additionally, **if you connect to your Medial Nature during times of transition, change, and endings, you will discover helpful and aligned insight that will lead you forward with ease to a stage of renewal and rebirth.**

Remember the entire task of retrieving the deer was initiated by Baba Yaga. Our old Wild Witch knew exactly what she was doing when she told the steward to send Fedot to retrieve the golden deer. The Wild Nature often kick-starts this initiation in order for us all to retrieve the Instinctual Self consciously, meaning that the Wild Nature will always initiate healing and change as necessary, whether it is required either on a personal or collective level—or both. We in turn then have the opportunity to flourish because of these changes, because we come into closer contact with our Instinctual Natures—our inner deer, so to speak.

Imagine if Anna, the interspecies communicator, had dismissed the Medial vision that she had. She would simply have returned to her old identity as a "regular" person and our leopard would have greatly suffered. Imagine if I dismissed my dreams and intuition, then this book would cease to exist, and you would never be reading these words. Imagine if you don't show us as your full self in this life. What a loss that would be. It requires courage to release old identities and patterns of being in order to truly step into your Soulful life and power, to show up authentically as who you really are, or at the least to give yourself the opportunity to discover who that is. It requires courage to cross this threshold in order to become a Wild Medial. To actually listen to soulful, wild, and oracular insight *and then take action because of it. To be as much part of that world as this one*, and to stand true in the reality of who you really are.

THE NECESSITY OF RETRIEVING WILD INSTINCTS

Now, ask any hunter and they will tell you that it is like deer have a sixth sense, that they can sniff out what is coming before it happens, and that they also know exactly how to zigzag when they are being stalked by a predator. Our instincts are the same—they are visceral and embodied. Your body can alert you to something before your conscious mind has even registered what is happening. A gut feeling, goose bumps, hairs on the back of your neck—your body often instinctively knows before "you" do. Yet here is the kicker: Our instincts, just like a deer's, are either absolutely enhanced or limited by years of handed-down programming and conditioning. That said, depending on your past experiences and how well you've already nurtured your instincts will influence what kind of healing work you need to do in order to restore them to optimal functioning. So many people have abandoned their instincts to the farthest kingdom in the 13th land because of too much societal and inner conditioning.

We are taught to bypass our embodied instincts over and over again by suppressing our Wild Natures: "Dress like this," "Speak like this," "Don't do this," "Only do that," and sometimes it's even more subtle than that. It can simply look like a parent or partner being more at ease when you are as they wish to see you. At this point in time, I also feel that so many people are already aware of this type of conditioning, yet they do not know what to do differently. They have forgotten how to reconnect to their own instinctive selves because it has been so long since they acted on their own inner kindling of knowing and sensing.

In relation to this, I remember watching an interview with world renowned violence-prevention expert Gavin de Becker on his book *The Gift of Fear: Survival Signs that Protect Us from Violence*. In the interview, he told the audience that he was motivated to write the book because he had repeatedly heard one common feature being shared by multiple survivors of crimes (sadly, mostly women) who shared their story. Almost every single survivor said that they knew—just knew—that something was **both intuitively and instinctively** wrong (although on the surface nothing appeared that way) before they fell victim to the crime that followed. Instead of honoring their instincts, they dismissed them, generally **over the fear of being impolite.**

The fear of being impolite is directly related to what happens when we squash our Wild Instincts and Medial Natures over and over again. And although this story is a hard-hitting example of what can go wrong when we become supremely disconnected from our Wild and instinctive natures, it also acts as a cautionary tale that teaches us the necessity of good instincts. (Equally, there is no blame here placed on anyone who is victimized.)

In contrast, just imagine if Baba Yaga, our old witch, were standing out on a street, when she sniffed out something that felt "off," like someone wanting to steal her handbag. She would absolutely turn around and stare the perpetrators down before they even had a chance to get close to her, and in the glint of her eye, they would recognize a warning that told them she was feral to the bone should they dare come closer. They would recognize that they were dealing with an Old Wolf whose hairs were standing up on the back of her neck, alerting her to danger, and that perhaps it was *they who should be concerned and not she*.

Instinct, the Wild Nature, and common sense go hand in hand—Baba Yaga would equally run if she knew she could not win. All three of these inner knowings must work together cohesively within you. There is also an important differentiating factor here that is worth mentioning, which is that aggression and Wild Instinct are not one and the same thing. Instinct nurtures and protects life, whereas aggression is often due to internalized and unregulated pain or suffering that is then outwardly aimed. Discernment and self-awareness are required here, as the first form of action is life-preserving, whereas the second is life-injuring.

If you often act in an aggressive manner that is not the Wild Nature, it's more likely pain within waiting to be witnessed and released. Perhaps this is why we also see an aspect of the instinctive principle in our fairy tale symbolized by a deer, because continuous priming of good instincts does not make us more aggressive; it actually makes us gentler but primed to act accordingly and in an instant if need be. Like when a normally gentle deer kicks a predator in the face if they come too close to their offspring, our instincts must be primed in the same way. They should be gentle, alert, but potent when necessary.

We see here again and again that good instincts protect life and do not result in injury or death as societal conditioning or fear dictates. In other words, when the dominant culture or society says, "If you don't behave like a good, polite, sweet little thing who thinks as we tell you to, well, then, bad things will happen." It is then when we must remember with our Wild selves that "No, this is not true!" If we act like polite little things at all times, that is when we lose our instincts, and then we truly are at risk. Equally, when we are too afraid to speak, that is when we are in serious danger. Anything that dictates that you cannot speak or think for yourself for fear of group retribution has fallen into shadow control. Similarly, we must reflect in order to see if we ourselves are falling into groupthink and behaving like a participant of a vicious pack cloaked in self-righteousness. Thankfully, the antidote for these obstacles is there for us: It is our Wild and Medial Natures.

In order to restore your instincts, you must free yourself from any internalized guilt or shame that is evoked when you act Instinctually. You cannot act like a sleeping beauty and think that everything will be okay when your instincts are screaming otherwise.

One of my teachers told me an experience they once had with a client who sought guidance as to whether she should leave her partner. Intuitively, he knew that something was wrong and asked her to show him her ear. She obliged, only to reveal that in a moment of rage, her partner had shot at her, aiming to hit the wall behind her but instead taking off part of her ear. That is how disconnected she had become from her own Instinctual Self—that even after losing her ear, she still doubted whether it was okay to protect herself. Luckily, my teacher did what was necessary in order to assist her in empowering herself.

We must summon our inner Baba Yaga and unleash her as necessary, but in order to do this, one's instincts must be sharpened time and again. On a more everyday level, that can simply look like eating nourishing foods without remorse. Enjoying pleasure. Moving your body in a way that feels good and saying no to what depletes you. It also looks like using your mind and speech wisely and compassionately and resting well nightly. It is in the repetitive honoring of our instinctive natures, which creates consistent well-being. Yet conditioned fear often gets in the way of this well-being because it is often underpinned by guilt, which is either internalized over many years of societal and cultural conditioning or from outright shaming in reaction to when one does act Instinctually. This is what squashes the Wild Nature. **The challenge, then, is to recognize when you feel guilt or shame in relation to your Instinctual "pings" and then alter that pattern consciously.**

You can break this knee-jerk pattern by seeing through the eyes of the Medial Nature on a regular basis. When you lift your perspective to that of Soul sight that says, "See your fear/guilt/shame for what it is and return it to an image of light—return to love, joy, and well-being." You can simply witness it and say, "Oh, this is just my guilt acting up because of what I was taught, but now I am Wild, wise, and free, so I choose again." Say this as many times as you need until it becomes truth embodied in your being. Flip the script, see things differently, forgive, pick another path. Over and over again, this is our challenge as human beings, to limit fear and turn toward well-being instead. To use our Soul sight hand in hand with our Instinctual natures to nurture wholeness. That said, though, if you feel like you are unwell Instinctually—that is, you feel like an echo or a whisper of who you truly are—then the antidote for this may simply be to reconnect with your Wild knowing through *your anger.*

I read a story of a woman who got to such a numb stage of living that she went home one day and burned her house down to the ground. I know a lot of people may also read that sentence and be well acquainted with that desire, but this is the extreme of what can happen when repression becomes the norm in everyday life. This is what happens when you or circumstances box you in to a life that you don't or no longer fit into.

The key to freedom here, then, begins with an interior uncaging.

Had that woman been able to address her own needs earlier and rekindle her Wild Nature in a healthier way, I believe that she could have avoided that situation. She symbolically could have burned down the inner structures that were imprisoning her and then taken good actions in her life to create real freedom. She could have trusted her Wild longing for change and listened to her Medial Nature for a pathway out of her pain and suffering. That takes more work than burning down a house as it requires wakeful vigilance. Striking the match of awareness daily by consciously choosing to show up and participate in the world in a way that feels authentic even when life and circumstances are hard.

The sad irony is that she ended up going to prison—a real cage. Although perhaps she felt freer—who's to say? Personally, I would want to be out in the big wide world, as I imagine she would too. I deeply feel for her because I know how easy it is to fall into despair when you feel like you don't have options, when every part of you is saying, *Enough!* **Yet that is when we must remember: I can use my Medial sight to perceive new options when my Wild Instinct screams, "This is not right."** Medial knowing will not lead you to harm; it will point you to the easiest exit so that you return to well-being. The Wild and Medial Natures must work hand in hand *within you.*

In order to do this, we must first acknowledge that Wild inner longings cannot be ignored or sidelined forever without consequence. When that happens, burning down the house seems like a very good idea. Secondly, we must remember that inner fire (anger, rage, frustration) actually points us in the direction of what needs healing and liberation. In other words, inner fire must be well tended to, or, as we've seen, it can become a blazing furnace of destruction. Thirdly, we must also be able to discern which structures must be let go of in their entirety. Every so often, that must also occur through the rapid fires of transformation so that hope can arise from the alchemical ashes. If that is the case, we must move forward confidently while remembering that while **Wild Woman alerts, Medial Woman directs. You will come out the other side anew.**

As I get older, I crave more loving and compassionate ways of instigating change for myself and others. Often, change is instigated when one is brutally honest with themselves, but that does not always mean that it should be followed by brutal actions. The Medial Nature shows us at those times how to return to our center and from that powerful space to make decisions. It is in the heart-space where we allow ourselves to change reality by first letting our true intentions reveal themselves. We understand that we must not run away from our lives but center ourselves in them consciously and mindfully while seeing the full picture—the full circle that we participate in and have created with our choices. From there, action is then helpful.

We must awaken our Medial hearts in relation to our Wild Natures. The heart provides nourishment; it fulfills real needs and understanding. It provides compassionate and wise decision-making that prevents leaving a wake of disaster behind you. A call to the heart shows us that, yes, there is a way to be Wild, loving, and free, to move through the different cycles and requirements of life with grace and equanimity. To replace old structures without needing to burn everything to the ground while equally allowing oneself to emanate peace during times of change. I also know that this sentiment sounds rather prescriptive, and that is not always easy or doable, but I ultimately mean it as an aim of contemplation. It is like reaching for a high ideal and hoping to hit it as opposed to waiting till such a level of frustration and pain occurs only to then instigate change ragefully.

If you have been pretending to be someone else and then all of a sudden show everyone who you are, you cannot be surprised that those people may be upset. This is not cause for fear—make those Wild changes as necessary, but keep your heart open toward yourself and others. You can hold space for both your side and their side of the story and still do what you need to do. This is also not the same thing as conceding to people who will never accept and love you for who you really are or who let you down consistently—in those cases, walking away is a kindness.

On a day-to-day basis, you can simply return to well-being by freely feeling and healthily expressing your emotions and needs, standing your ground as needed, and allowing the water to move over you as it wakes up your sense of touch. These are just a few things that can help get you started. Equally, if you follow your own Wild promptings, you will be well on your way in no time. Then perhaps one day you will wake up as a dear Old Wolf—one who is both gentle and formidable. In the meantime, here are a few modern traps to watch out for that habitually deplete both the Wild and Medial Natures:

- Allowing a persona to direct your life decisions.
- Junk food that dulls the senses and numbs the body.
- Too much TV, news, and social media that floods the mind and senses, relegating intuition to the sidelines.
- Sustained fearmongering, which creates fatigue, polarization, and disharmony.
- Rigid thinking, which creates separation and internalized fear.

- Performative living, which creates inner conflict.
- Internalized narratives replayed over and over again due to childhood conditioning.
- Boxing yourself in to an old story or way of being and not doing anything about it.
- Excessive focus on other people's needs to the detriment of your own or vice versa.
- Doing the same old thing in a relationship and not recognizing that you and/or the other person have changed.

When you first begin to do practices in order to reclaim your Wild and Medial self, you may very well feel like you are someone who is learning to walk their talk. As it is in the *practice of doing* that the healing happens, not in the talking, thinking, or performative posting of the doing, which is Wild mimicry—#SoulCrushing. People may call you weird, like the old hag who lives in the deep dark woods, but you must draw a line in the sand in order to return to well-being. Where you demand that this is what is allowed and no more. You also don't need to perform massive feats to transform. A little action done day after day goes a long way. Waking up every morning and meditating for five minutes for guidance is good enough. Walking in mindfulness every time you move is good enough. Dropping in to your Medial heart daily so you can hear your Soul is good enough. Choosing to be kind when it is easier to blow things up is good enough. Being honest with yourself when it is easier to pretend otherwise is good enough.

These practices, when done consistently, will help you remain clear about what it is that you will allow in your life and house—including the house of your psyche. Ultimately, we must accept what we need and be who we unequivocally are, as that is the true medicine that affords us the greatest healing. And please don't pretend just because it may be easier to fit in. Perhaps you were born to live on the edges as a trailblazer, one who can sense a hunter from many miles away, so that you can teach others to do the same.

Let us now circle back to that earlier interview with trailblazer and violence-prevention expert Gavin de Becker, who helps people avoid becoming victims of the hunters of society. I found it so interesting to learn that he wrote his book to help teach people the importance of honoring their instincts and intuition while also acknowledging the profound gift that visceral fear can provide in life-threatening situations, an unlikely one that can easily be taken for granted. Perhaps in a different vein but built off the bedrock of his sentiment, one of the reasons I wrote this book was in the hopes that you would come to remember that you are one with both the Medial and Wild parts of you and that natural fear and conditioned fear are two entirely different things.

The remedy, then, is that when you honor the Wild Nature within you, you are able to sniff out the predator of the mind as well as the predator of society, both of which feed off fear, whether perceived or real. Then, when you simultaneously honor the Medial Nature within you, you willingly release conditioned fear in order to step in to the glorious unknown. Together, the Wild and Medial Natures show you which fear is helpful and which is binding. It is up to you to then remember that when both the Wild Woman and Medial Woman are strong and vitally alive within you, so are you.

WILD VISION AND ACCEPTING SOUL GIFTS

We must return now to the mythic realm of Blue Dove and Fedot, for the Medial and the Wild require greater integration—as do we. As you know, at the last point in our story, we saw that Blue Dove had retrieved the golden deer for Fedot, and he in turn gave it to the king because he had to. Analytically, we could say that the Ego Self has come into contact with the

Instinctual Self through the Medial Nature, but at this point the instinct is still in service to the tyranny of the mind or society. We know this because the deer has been given to the king.

As the journey progresses, we learn that the king is actually highly displeased with this turn of events because he doesn't want the deer. What he really wants is Fedot out of the picture so that he can claim Blue Dove as his own. In other words, he wants total dominion over the Medial Nature. He wants to use her Soulful insight and knowing for his own benefit. In reaction to his own unhappiness, he unleashes his rage onto the steward by giving him an ultimatum: Either come up with a plan to really get rid of Fedot or there will be hell to pay! In turn, the steward returns to Baba Yaga, and this is what she advises:

> Fear not. We will give them a difficult problem, one that is not so easy to solve. Tell the King to send Fedot to the land of "I know not where" and bring back "I know not what." That is the true edge of destruction, where Shmat-Razum lives. He will not complete the task in all eternity, as he will fail or get lost, so your problem will be solved either way![6]

How curious that our Wild old hag would send Fedot to the edge of destruction on what seems like an absolute goose chase to find Shmat-Razum. Who or what is a Shmat-Razum, even? Good grief! And how does this even relate to you sitting in your current space-time reality? Well, as you will come to see, it's all about Wild Vision. That is the Wild and Medial ability to see that which lies beyond form and object—to see what is beyond this very physical world of perception that we all participate in—in order to restore it.

Baba Yaga teaches us how to stay awake so we can recognize the Soul in all its different forms, and she also teaches us about what happens when we fail to see with Wild Vision. We learn about the loss that occurs both within us and in the outside world, where we lose nature. When the Medial and Wild are relegated to the sidelines we collectively end up at the true edge of destruction just like our poor Fedot. Ouch! We know this in our heart of hearts—that circumstances in the outside world feel like they are out of balance, and that perhaps before this time, one could get away with not witnessing the collective upheaval. Yet here we are, where it is near impossible to pretend that things are not awry and that we are potentially all on a collective quest whether we consciously acknowledge this or not.

And so Fedot goes home deeply saddened after hearing about this second unwanted task that has been forced upon him, just as I imagine so many of us feel like when confronting world news or personal problems and/or patterns of inherited pain. In response to this unwanted experience, he tells Blue Dove what has happened, and once more she tells him to go to sleep so that she can go outside and practice her magic. Once again, Medial magic can only be instigated when the Ego Self sleeps, and we will explore how to honor this practice in the upcoming chapters. But for now, let us return to Blue Dove, who in her true form summons the two youths, who appear, but this time they cannot solve the problem for her. They do not know where Shmat-Razum lives, and so here we see a kind of plot twist in our story.

Is the Medial Nature unable to solve this problem? On the surface it may seem so, but we are required to dive in further, and as we do, we discover that before her husband sets on his way, Blue Dove gives him two gifts. The first gift is a ball, and the second is a piece of cloth. Both gifts are of her own making—in other words, they are gifts connected to the Soul that can be accessed through the Medial Nature at any point.

Later we come to discover that these Medial gifts help Fedot immensely on his journey, and so perhaps the task is not for the Medial Woman to solve the problem entirely, but rather for her husband (the Ego Self) to find his own connection to the Medial world and his Soulful nature. This is in a way the quest within the quest, one that is required of all of us.

We also discover a larger quest that is experienced on a collective level. We collectively need to restore Wild Nature, respect one another's differences, and return to a balanced way of being. At the same time the interior journey is one of Soul remembrance. It is learning how to deeply connect with your Soul on a daily basis through the Medial Nature so that your personal life can expand beautifully while also helping to heal the collective by focusing awareness on Wild well-being. Together the quest within the quest weaves wholeness for everyone through you.

Through us.

The story tells us, "Let your life's direction be Soul-led." You can roll that "Medial ball" as often as you need. For our purposes a Medial ball is really any tool that can aid you in communing with your Soul directly, like sitting in silence, dream practices, oracle cards, or deep meditation. You can seek Soulful direction before taking any step forward on your quest, even if you are just going to the supermarket. And when you are there, you may recognize with your Soul sight—that is, your Wild vision—that food isn't just food.

That the seed that lies in the apple is what recreates the next generation of trees and sustenance. And that it doesn't take anything other than our willingness and a bit of water and soil to give a seed a chance to come to life as a fruitful tree, that it may very well be the mirrored Tree of Life and not just for you but for your community and the generations that will come after you are gone. Perhaps a visit to the supermarket can even remind us that just like trees that were once seeds, so, too, were we something else before we materialized into physical life and that we are still these things. Seemingly mundane experiences are deeply imbued with blessings of grace and well-being when you begin to perceive them with your Soul sight.

Now we circle back to Fedot, who has embarked on his quest so that we can learn more about this mythic journey, and we see that the king responds by sending for Blue Dove and forcefully demanding that she become his wife. "If you do not come willingly, then I will take you by force."[7] To which Blue Dove laughs and then turns into a bird and simply flies out the window.

I love this part of the story not because of the vile violence and domination but because it reminds me that the Medial Nature cannot be forced, controlled, or dominated. The story tells us that although the physical body and the mind can be dominated the Soul cannot be forced. The feminine nature has been severely abused throughout time, and the earth, too—we collectively have pillaged and overused her—and yet here we see the garnering of a higher form of perception: The Soul is incorruptible, both our own and that of the world's.

The Medial Nature is able to laugh in the face of tyranny, suffering, or over-egoic demands while it changes into a bird and flies out the window. Yet we must call these Soul birds back to ourselves. We must open the windows of our minds and allow the Soul to come back and steer both our individual and collective direction. Here we see that we are now in the realm of Soul retrieval. In this space, we are tasked to recover the parts of ourselves that we have lost for whatever reason—pain, suffering, heartbreak, disappointment, or trauma. Whatever caused the Soul to take flight and exit from the realm of the here and now must return to us, as we collectively need to act from a more integrated and centered place.

When we do this, we receive a huge flood of vital energy. That is because the intrapsychic energy that has gone into repressing or containing unwanted things is now released to be of use elsewhere and in a better way. Shamanically speaking, Soul retrieval is not symbolic. It is a very real act in which the Soul is called back to the individual so that they can feel and be better. It demands a removal of energetic blocks, and it also requires an excavation of the unconscious—mining it for what has caused the loss of the Soul in the first place in order to restore everything back to wholeness. When we work with the unconscious, we are able to dive into the hidden motivators and painful, repressed, or ancient stories of the past that bind one to a half-alive life, equally, then, restoring these to well-being.

The Soul, Medial Self, Wild Vision—these things are also not just metaphors; they are all aspects of our nonphysical selves that we can actively connect with. Anyone who has had a profound meditative experience, inner knowings, lucid dreams, or even a near-death experience will know what I mean. It stops being theoretical and becomes experiential. That is part of the discovery during the quest and journey—that is, to move from an idea to a belief to a form of deep knowing. Like when your body gets goose bumps and there is no way to unknow what you know. It's about experiencing these things for yourself in a way that fits for where your current level of awareness is while embracing the journey.

In my own journey, I had the good fortune when I was training to become a psychologist to additionally study with many metaphysical teachers. This type of seemingly opposing training was immensely helpful. In both the therapy room and outside under the sky, the Soul can return. All paths lead to wholeness, and mostly, in my experience, we pick the paths we identify with—those that lend to our already internalized and established set of beliefs. We gravitate to what we find most palatable. Yet, in my opinion, good practitioners from whatever direction are able to facilitate a gateway through which you can walk because your willingness to heal, to cross the bridge or mend the divide, has already been intended, just like how a book can become a gateway that leads you straight to your heart and healing. Like the old adage tells us, when you are ready, what you need will appear.

CHAPTER 7

ROLL THAT MEDIAL BALL UNTIL YOU LAND *IN THE* WILD WOODS

There is a wonderful condition of fairy tales and myth, which is that everything has reason and meaning, even if that meaning is meant for another time period altogether. After all, this fairy tale marriage between Blue Dove and Fedot was written in the 1800s and is well over two hundred years old, spilling medicine for our modern times. So, in the end who's to know when a story is finished or when Blue Dove and Baba Yaga are done with us? Perhaps *they do*.

Let us now reenter into that hut of mythic time, where we see that Fedot has been on a very long quest. His journey has been treacherous, disheartening, even, and yet he perseveres. Endurance is the long game at this point in time. He is wandering and wandering, as do we in the same way over the terrain of our lives. Yet, with some luck, he stumbles onto a witch's hut in the deep dark woods. And by virtue of you reading this story, you, too, have entered into the enchantment of that Wild hut and are now meeting Baba Yaga directly, word by word. May she be woven in full form within your psyche by the end of this book.

Here we take a great step in our mythic initiation as Fedot has finally met the Wild Woman directly, which means we have as well. We have taken a great step in our mythic initiation, as it was previously only the steward who was meeting Baba Yaga on backward roads and in wasted places. In other words, the Ego Self was connecting with the Wild Nature in a foolish manner—out of the Wilderness in a backward way and in sheer panic. Now we see that the intention and motivation within the psyche has changed and that there has been **helpful and important inner movement.** That the psyche is now shifting away from egoic impulses and toward greater balance and integration. This is the equivalent of allowing your Ego Self to take a back seat while you follow one Medial step after another until you meet Wild Woman directly. You may want to pause here in order to reflect on *how and when* you choose to connect to both your Medial and Wild abilities.

Do you use your Medial abilities to connect in service to things outside of you, like your community, nature, the Spirit of the land? Or do you only connect when you are panicked and in fear? How about when you are so set on something that you can't think straight? Or when you are calm and centered or a combination of all these things?

As you've seen throughout our story, we can connect with the Wild, Instinctual, and Medial Natures at any point even through unlikely emotions like fear. Yet helpful and aligned action is almost always easier sought through centered petitioning, **as intentional grace is the gateway to gaining Medial awareness.** We must surrender our small thoughts that constrain higher consciousness in order to be led. In order to do this, we must first root our perception in compassion for self and others, which clears the channel from egoic noise. The Ego Self must learn to step aside so that the Medial connection can be made in order for you to receive divine guidance.

Here's another way of approaching this. Have you ever wanted something so desperately that you picked up an oracle deck and asked whether you would receive what you wanted, only to then receive guidance that you didn't want to hear? So, you reshuffled the cards with the hopes of the answer changing, *but it didn't*. This kind of behavior is steward-esque in nature. The steward would drive forward regardless of what the Instinctual Self advises. Whereas, at this point in the story, a more mature self would listen to the guidance they received, knowing that it is immensely valuable regardless of hoped-for outcomes. They would know from experience that the guidance was pointing them to something better or simply showing them information that they were missing from their current point of view.

It bodes well for us to listen closely and heed the good advice we receive when we are in the proverbial witch's hut. After all, why would you go on a whole journey to discover the Wild and Medial within you only to then dismiss the guidance you receive? You wouldn't! It is important to seek higher guidance from a place that is heart-centered as opposed to only seeking it during times of obsessive thinking or wanting. This creates a respectful dialogue between you and the unseen. It creates reverence for your ability to even be able to connect in the first place—to have the gift of Medial abilities.

As our folktale continues, Baba Yaga then offers Fedot food and shelter, and we discover that the Wild within can offer us both refuge and sustenance when we come into direct contact with it. Fedot in turn accepts Baba Yaga's food, and then, as always, he takes out the cloth that Blue Dove gave him, and he wipes his face with it. Baba Yaga's eyes sharpen when she sees the cloth and her voice becomes shrill: "That is my sister's!"[1]

This is a great moment disguised in simplicity, as the Wild Nature has now recognized the Medial Nature. Meaning that the Wild Nature is now consciously connected with the oracular nature. We in turn then recognize and honor them as Soulfully connected within our own psyche. We acknowledge that they are a thread woven over time and so let it once again be known that where there is one Wild Sister, there is a Medial close by.

We must also acknowledge that we have been dealing with a **triadic bond** between the Ego Nature, Medial Nature, and Wild Nature that has just become conscious within one individual.

What this means for you is that if you follow this journey of initiation, you will become aware of the gifts and weaknesses associated with each nature. Sometimes your heart will require you to reach down to your roots to rediscover the Wild Woman. Other times it will tell you to free yourself from being earthbound so that you can receive higher insight—so that you can become a conduit between worlds, a Modern Medial. Eventually you will come to walk with both women beside you, and at the same time, you will also come to be more at peace with your ego nature. You will know exactly how to quiet your mind so that you can open your magic book (communing with the unseen) when you need to. But before you can do that, you need to know which step you are on in this journey. Let us reflect on the initiatory steps we have taken up until this moment. Try to recognize where you are in the process.

Step 1: The Ego Self is initiated on an unwanted quest.

Something outside of you knocks you onto a path of inner awakening and knowing. This is likely very disruptive to your ego identity/small self. Sometimes it can happen through a spontaneous awakening of awareness, like if you randomly hear Spirit when you are driving your car. Other times, it often happens when you are met with unwanted change, like through a crisis. This can also happen multiple times in a person's life.

Step 2: The Ego Self makes contact with the Medial Nature, but it is early days.

You receive higher flashes of insight and spontaneous knowing, but you do not know how to consciously and easily connect to this "intuitive channel" on a regular basis, nor do you always follow the advice that you receive.

Step 3: The Medial Nature provides two Soul gifts of its own making: Medial direction (in our tale, the ball) and Medial cleansing (the cloth).

Your Medial Nature shows you which way to go to move with the Soul. It equally shows you what you need to cleanse, nurture, and release on a habitual basis for well-being. We can and should use these Soul gifts throughout the journeys of our lives.

Step 4: Acceptance of Medial gifts leads the Ego Self to the wise Wild Nature: Instinctual knowing and sensing.

You are truthful with yourself and release any untruths that bind you to a half-alive life. These truths are often upsetting to the Ego Self but awaken the instincts that can return you to well-being.

Step 5: The Wild Nature in turn recognizes the Medial Nature (the oracular and precognitive function of the psyche).

Instinctual knowing becomes linked with oracular knowing. You have a gut feeling to turn left when you usually go right. The Wild Nature alerts you to danger, and the Medial directs you on your Soul's path. At this step we can intimately discover that the Medial Nature is ever present in thresholds and that the Wild Nature is present in every cycle (life/death/life). Here we also come to accept that new beginnings often arise from the radical acceptance of being in the in-between.

Ultimately, this mythic journey is an initiation that helps to integrate three forms of perception. Ego Sight is mundane perception. Medial Sight is oracular perception. Wild Sight is Instinctual perception. All three are connected through your greater awareness, seeing with each perception when and as is necessary so that you can consciously move between the realms of the seen and the unseen—the past, present, and future.

When you are lost, feel defeated, and can't seem to find your way, the Medial Woman can guide you. She is Mother Mystery, and she will help you to develop night vision so that you may become fluent in the language of dreams and psychic knowings. She will teach you how to willingly close your ego eyes, to center in stillness, so that you can receive Soul-guided insights. She will also help you to mine the treasures of the unconscious offering you Medial direction as you dive into the depths of that which is not easily seen but which has influence. She will help you witness what is hidden from your awareness, bringing it to light, and in turn removing its fated outcome.

If you find yourself detached and lost from that which nurtures you, that which is life-giving, then send out a howl to Wild Woman, and she will revive you. She will unleash your creative impulses and light a fire to that which has become cold and deadened. She will instigate necessary change through every Wild longing and ferocious knowing. When Wild Woman walks topside, she can be felt every time your body knows without knowing. Ultimately, when all three forms of seeing (Ego Sight, Instinctual Sight, Medial Sight) are in harmony, you will discover you already hold all the resources you need to move forward, and what you need will appear before you as if brought to you by the ether.

Let us now detour into another story entirely to see how this triadic bond can work well together. Let us peer into rural Virginia, in an altogether different time-space reality: If one would watch her from far away like we are doing right now, they would see a young woman working in the fields. She is sweating. Laboring. Moving with the earth. And that is when she hears it: an echo of air barreling across the horizon, carrying words with it.

The earth beneath her begins to tremble, and by virtue of this she knows—*just knows*—that there is only one response she can make. And that is to run—and *to run like hell*. Moving swiftly toward her home, words right behind her, she must make it to pen and paper. If she makes it home in time, she will grab hold of the words tightly until they are put down on paper. But if she doesn't make it home in time, well, then, the words simply barrel forward, moving with the wind, scanning the field for another receptive oracle to bring them to life. Every so often she only catches the words by their tail end, having failed to run home fast enough. And in those moments, she pulls them back into her body while scribing them onto the page. Delightfully, the words come out perfectly but written backward—from the very last word to the first. The result: a perfect poem in all its forms.

It may surprise you to know that this is a true story of the prolific American poet Ruth Stone, who shared her creative process with Elizabeth Gilbert in a private meeting. Gilbert then graced the world with a version of this story in a TED Talk.[2] Now, imagine if Ruth Stone hadn't ran home in order to catch these Wild Medial knowings, these gifts. Then we would have lost out on her rich and meaningful works.

And so, how do we come to stop, look, and listen in a way that stirs the Soul and awakens our senses to the fact that we are alive right now? We evoke our triadic perception and come to trust that, as Stone knew, we can hear intuitive whispers and the words in the willows. The ones sent by Wild Woman herself, beckoning us to unleash our creative selves, our true Selves, if we are simply brave enough to run home.

We all have the ability to see and hear while we labor in the Wild fields of our lives. Yet it is up to each one of us to trust in our Medial ways, where divine gifts are received and not thought. When Stone was writing, in those very moments she was a Medial Woman—a bridge between worlds, a conduit for divine inspiration. Now, even if you have not grabbed hold of any poems lately, this way of being and receiving already exists within you. You simply need to *surrender.* When that happens, the poem is brought to the poet, the answer finds the question, and the seeker meets the guide.

CHAPTER 8

WHEN ALL HOPE IS LOST *AND* RETURNING HOME

Let us return to our fairy tale to see our story through where Baba Yaga has just met with Fedot. And in response, he tells her about his unwanted quest to go to the edge of destruction to find Shmat-Razum. With the full force of her strength, Baba Yaga summons all the animals and birds in the entire land. "Do any of you know where Shmat-Razum can be found?"[1] But no one knows. So, she goes to her magic book, and in an instant two giants appear. "What dost thou need, dear?"

Here we see the parallel between Blue Dove and Baba Yaga—they both tap into the same Spiritual and benevolent power source when they are petitioned for help by the Ego Self. They *both* open their magic books, and two helpers appear. In the beginning of this story, Blue Dove opens her book and two youths appear, whereas when Baba Yaga opens her book and two giants appear. Here we see inner development and personal growth. Blue Dove is a Medial maiden at the beginning of the story, meaning that she is relatively new to her Medial gifts, whereas Baba Yaga is more seasoned, wiser, and more accustomed to her magic, so two giants appear. Baba Yaga's connection to the unseen is stronger because she has worked with it for a longer period of time.

As you use both your Medial and Wild Nature, you will equally discover this for yourself—you will become a more seasoned practitioner, and as such, both your Instinctual and intuitive abilities will become giant in nature. We will discover these abilities in the upcoming chapters. Let's return now to our story, where Baba Yaga says to her two giant helpers,

"My faithful helpers, take this traveler and me to the ocean and stop in the middle above the very abyss."[2]

I could write a whole book about that one sentence, but for now, let us return to the basics: The ocean is symbolic of the intrapsychic realm of the unconscious. It can also represent the watery nature of what we call the flow state, as well as our connection to unseen realms that we tap into through our Medial and intuitive abilities. In response, the two giants take Fedot and Baba Yaga and hold them up like two giant pillars hovering above the watery abyss. Imagine the Ego Self as one pillar, the Wild Self as another pillar, and the water below as the intuitive depths of the unconscious, the abyss of what cannot be seen but that which holds influence and knowing.

Suspended over the abyss, the Instinctual Self asks all the water creatures, "Know any of you where Shmat-Razum is and how to find him?" The Ego Self does not speak—it knows by now that it is best to listen here. The water creatures respond, but they do not know where Shmat-Razum lives. Then, just as Baba Yaga and Fedot are about to lose **all hope**, a very old frog suddenly appears. Currently, it is easy to feel hopeless about so many realities, yet our frog of hope appears just in time. She is so old and tiny that her body looks small and frail, but we see that her inner strength is immense. As the story tells us:

Kwa-kwa, *our old frog croaks. "I know where to find him, but I am far too old to leap there." Baba Yaga responds, "Fear not, Fedot. Take this glass of milk and place this frog within it—carry her to where she tells you to go."*

Through the animated balance of the Ego, Wild, and Medial Natures, we discover a helper from the center of the abyss—an old frog. That is the archaic and ancient retrieval of balanced knowing, being, and living. She is the oracle at the center, and she symbolically represents our ability to access the storehouse of all information held in the depths of the unconscious. Fedot places the frog in the milk (a symbol of nurturance and sustenance) and listens to her instruction. In other words, when we nurture, sustain, and respect the archaic wisdom that arises from the center of the abyss, we are then given the ability to cross any threshold safely.

In our story, our old frog takes him to the edge of the river and tells him to jump on her back. Fedot doubts himself and the situation for a moment. She is so small, a frail frog. How will she carry him? Yet, knowing well enough, he does what he is told, and she begins to grow and grow in size. Notice here that she doesn't first become big so that he can jump on her back. No, Fedot is required to trust and jump even when she looks like a small and frail thing to him. He is required once again to take a leap in faith, and as he does, she then expands in influence.

We understand at this point that the Ego Self may have its doubts, but it knows better than to doubt the helpful albeit cryptic guidance that it is receiving. **When applied to you and your life's journey, it is learning over and over again to trust in the archaic knowing that arises from your own inner depths and to let that guidance carry you on its back**, while also being acutely aware that this knowing is accurately retrieved when Wild Sight and Ego Sight are held in perfect equilibrium, just like two giants gracefully hovering over water.

Here we must also acknowledge that although Baba Yaga is old in our story, our frog is ancient—she lives in the water at the center of the abyss. *Our Wild Witch goes to her for help.* Herein lies the difference between the woods and the water in this story. Here the woods signify the land, the earth, Wild consciousness, whereas the water signifies the unconscious and the mystical and Medial realms of the unseen. Remember, we are dealing with archaic primal forces of which we cannot see the entire picture through our Ego Lens. So, we must trust in each step even if our rational minds cannot understand what is happening. And at the same time, we are required to have reverence for the fact that we can deliberately weave the mystical into the material with the help of these forces, that we can move Medially between the woods and the waters with our growing and expanding awareness of both.

Bridges, rivers, passageways, doorways—all these symbolic markers both in dreams and stories often show us that we ourselves need to cross over thresholds in order to move forward. They show us that a new form of consciousness is being initiated—that we are being initiated. Fedot and our old frog cross the threshold, and then she leaves him with a parting instruction: "At this river's edge lies a mountain, which you can see. Inside this mountain is a cave, which you cannot see, and in there you will find Shmat-Razum."

I imagine that Fedot is so damn relieved at this point—his journey has been long and exhausting—and there may just be a light in that cave for him. The mountain here symbolizes a higher perspective that can be accessed by entering the cave of stillness (going inward). When Fedot is in there, he quiets down and simply watches what happens. He becomes the observer, and it is there where he sees Shmat-Razum, who is a genie of sorts. He sees that the genie is in service to two highly disrespectful and greedy men barking demands at him. "Bring us food! Bring us wine! Yadda yadda!" He does as they demand, and eventually the two greedy men leave the cave.

Astonishingly, the name Shmat-Razum means "common sense." Fedot, whose name means "given by God," travels all the way to the edge of destruction to retrieve common sense. On the journey he discovers how important it is to listen to and be led by the Wild and Medial Nature. He then finally enters the cave of stillness and becomes an observer. In the stillness of perception, he witnesses the players within him that are in excess, the overinflated and hyper demanding aspects that result in greed and suffering in the external world.

This old folktale teaches us that when we lose our connection to our common sense, we inevitably end up at the edge of destruction—a place where it becomes necessary that we find that common sense again. Ecologically speaking, we are just a few mythic minutes away from disaster. So our collective task is then to use our common sense to safeguard our earth—to protect the Wild—and in doing so we safeguard ourselves. We must use common sense anytime we step out onto a destructive ledge because of excessive wants that damage our personal lives and/or the world at large. This is what heals the balance between things.

Through our story we rediscover that the Wild Nature is a blend of Soul sense and common sense, and the Medial Nature is a blend of Spirit sense and future knowing.

In our times a new path forward will need to be mapped by Medial solutions. In that our future lies not in going backward but in using the technology mindfully to bring balance and restore harmony, to find the center between old cyclical community ways of living and being while also accepting the fact that we are leaping into the future with technology. We must use our Medial sight (Spirit sense and future knowing) to map a way back to the Wild—as well as to one another. We have to remember our intrinsic link to all of life. That each choice holds a consequence that spreads out into the web of creation and influences life itself.

One less plastic cup in the ocean is a small example of this. Respecting nature and treating all its living creatures as sentient are good examples of how micro changes can affect the macrocosm. Choosing self-nurturing actions instead of harmful activities is a good example of this. It all goes hand in hand—the individual within the collective. The collective made up of all the individuals. We must sow balance for our time of extremes and when things shift again in the far-off future—we will hover in stillness above the center of the abyss and discover the next best way forward.

In the last leg of our mythic story, Fedot approaches Shmat-Razum and offers him food. They eat together, and as a result of Fedot's **kindness**, he chooses to leave with him. They have another mythic journey returning home where Shmat-Razum creates gifts straight from the ether—he is a genie, after all! They make sure they visit the old witch and the old frog in order to graciously thank them, knowing well enough that Fedot would have died a long time ago without their help.

Then at last they finally return to the kingdom, and Blue Dove, our Medial Woman, returns in full force. Fedot and Blue Dove reunite in strength and love toward each other. The original king is so outraged at the turn of events that he wages a war against them. In other words, the tyranny of the mind and culture do not give up easily even when balance between the Medial, Wild, Ego, and common sense is being restored. In other words, this is a symbolic message telling us to stay awake and lucid in our lives—to acknowledge that integrated wisdom requires wakeful alertness both personally and collectively. That balance is not static; it requires wakeful vigilance. Nevertheless, Fedot and Blue Dove overthrow the king, and the entire realm thrives as they rule together. As queen, Blue Dove now stands more fully in her strength and power. She is no longer an injured, half-alive bird shot down by the sharpshooter of life, she is now an empowered Mediatrix—noble and royal as she mediates with an open heart and mind for the well-being of all. Ultimately, Fedot and Blue Dove shine together and as a result the entire realm flourishes.

And with that, our initiation comes full circle.

So, in closing this journey, we must acknowledge that this story was one of death and rebirth, a gathering of lost parts that required both integration and transmutation. We looked to the earth for answers, and we met the Wild Witch. We remembered her as the One Who Knows so that we could recognize her as our inner kin. We discovered the oracle at the center of the abyss, our Medial Crone—Kwa-Kwa—and in our heart of hearts we know that she holds another story for us. And when the time is right for that story to be told I will unwind her watery threads so that we can dive into the abyss together. But for now, we must celebrate in the knowing that what was once lost has been found. Where there was discord, harmony now reigns true. And like all good things, we must accept that life is movement and that we must move right along with it. So, take the next step with me. Come and witness how to stand in strength, as both the silence and stillness are ready to witness you.

CHAPTER 9

IN THE SILENCE, *THE* ORACLE SPEAKS

In a sacred oak grove in the Greece of antiquity, an oracle walks barefoot. Her temple is made of the earth and the sky. She is known as the Oracle of Dodona, and she shows us how to listen with Medial ears in order to hear the Soul through the medium of the earth. She is the oldest-known oracle found in Greece, dating back to the second millennium B.C.E.—predating the Oracle of Delphi. It is said that she would sit beside an oak tree and listen to the leaves rustling in the wind, and from those sounds she would receive divine answers. In some ways this is similar to our poet Ruth Stone, who heard words barreling through the ether. It seems the air is a channel that we can all tune in to.

Herodotus, a famous historian, spoke to three priestesses from Dodona, who were called the peleiades (the word *peleiades* meaning "doves" in ancient Greek). And from his conversation with them, we have some information as to how this sanctuary came to be. He was told that two black doves (Egyptian priestesses) were exiled from Thebes. As a result, one went to Libya to the Siwa oasis and became the Oracle of Ammon and was also known as the oracle's sibyl (seer). The other went to Epirus in Greece and became the Oracle of Dodona and was also known as the voice of the oracle. In later mythology it was even said that a small piece of that very oak tree was incorporated into the ship *Argo*, and as a result the crew would receive prophetic warnings because of it. The oak tree and the oracle were linked together even over a far distance, just as you are intrinsically linked to your Medial Nature no matter how distant you feel from it.

As for Dodona, and as history tends to go, first the Aetolians invaded and destroyed the grounds in 219 B.C.E. Many years later King Philip V of Macedon restored the sanctuary and reconstructed the buildings, but then the Romans invaded and intentionally decimated the site again, after which Emperor Augustus then restored it once more. And as usual time kept weaving and with it so did the history of Dodona, and yet through all the change and turbulence people still came to visit the oracle. That is, until Emperor Theodosius came into power and shut all the temples down and ordered that the last surviving oak tree be cut down. Although there is one oak there now, it is my heart's wish that those who caretake for the site reforest an entire grove there. Perhaps we could help them with this endeavor.

When I picture the Oracle of Dodona, I imagine all the people that would travel to see her. I imagine them seeking her counsel, and I try to picture what they may have been experiencing. Was it love, heartbreak, confusion? Wonderfully, "regular" people were also allowed to visit the oracle. We know this because at the site archaeologists have uncovered hundreds of lead sheets with "everyday" questions carved on them. In fact, if you search for the acropolis museum and type in *Dodona*, you can see these inscriptions for yourself. But in the meantime, here are a few real questions (some of which are heartbreaking) that were asked:

"Is this deep winter caused by a transgression by one of us?" "What is better for me: to pay my debts now or later?" "I am Kittos, slave of Dionysios, and I ask: Will he set me free as he promised?" "It is Myrta speaking to you and I want to know if I will become a widow." "Will I, the ship, and my cargo be safe on the voyage to Carthage?" "Should I go with another man to have children?"[1]

We all seek answers for different reasons, and just like the people of histories past, we are somehow set in the time periods we find ourselves in. Our modern-day questions to the oracle may now sound like this: "Is AI a gift or curse?" And in the next breath we might ask, "Will I get what I want?" Just like the people of ancient times, we, too, find ourselves asking about larger sociopolitical influences as well as our personal questions. We are seeking answers as to how things will blend for the collective as well as for ourselves personally. Especially now, when we are bombarded with so much information that it is often hard to know what is really true. Yet, in order for us to intuit both the smaller and larger answers, we must commune with the oracle within us. And in order to do that, we must first create the sacred space needed for the Medial Nature to flourish.

There are many ways to create sacred space, but here are two broader options—one is an interior method, and the other is a physical one. When you return to your heart, you drop into the sacred space that already exists within you, and when you return to nature, you immerse yourself in the sanctuary of what is naturally sacred. Both of these methods can open up the oracular nature within you. The Medial Nature flourishes out in nature and within the psyche. As such, **the heart and nature are both complimentary activators of your oracular abilities.**

Anytime that you find yourself in nature, you are in a sacred space. The wind is sacred, and it speaks to you when you are still enough to hear it. The sky is sacred, and it will lift your perspective higher when you engage your Medial sight with it. The earth is holy, even if it is layered with concrete, as beneath it is the living, breathing element of life itself. When you choose to go into nature, in a sacred manner, you come closer to the oracle, and as a result the elements mirror guidance to you. Equally, if you deliberately create sacred space within you, that is when intuitive and psychic insights can come directly to you—either through sacred hearing (clairaudience) or sacred seeing (clairvoyance), as well as other methods of intuitive perceiving.

Have you ever seen the movie *Field of Dreams*? It's a somewhat unexpected example, but illustrates the point. In the film, Kevin Costner plays the role of a farmer who builds a baseball field on his land because he hears a disembodied voice that tells him to. The following adapted line from the movie is now quite famous: "If you build it, they will come." In the story, the ghosts of baseball legends start to appear and play games on that field. Later, his father also visits him there, and a great form of healing happens. Everything heals: the outside, the inside, and in Spirit.

Spirit/higher consciousness needs a space to be heard. It needs the ego mind to quiet down, to be hushed into contemplative stillness so that it can clearly share its insights. It needs you to build your own version of a "baseball field" so that you can be in communion with the Spirit world. In this sense, sleep is a naturally Medial space—it is quite literally (although not physically) a sacred field of dreams. This is just one of the reasons as to why dreams are so powerful and why people often have experiences with disembodied voices just as they are waking up, because they are finally quiet enough to *listen*. Spirit is always speaking, but finally, there is enough space, enough room for guidance to be heard, for the Medial aspects of life to take precedence.

One of the first questions I usually get asked in relation to this is "How can I cultivate this sacred space so that I can hear with my Medial ears and eyes?" In response, the practices that I recommend are not fancy. They are not shiny or bespoke. They are part earthen-made as well as Spirit-woven—a blend of the two very things we collectively need most now. And they are yours for the taking. So, how do you return to your center and create sacred space in waking life in order to receive oracular insights?

You get very quiet and very still.

Stillness and silence—the two keys to the interior castle, and yet it is so hard to often put these things into practice. One literally just needs to get still and quiet down any mental chatter and/or external noise! In our modern times technology can be a huge distraction in this sense. So please become mindful as you reach for your phone or if you find yourself returning to a memory of pain, try to bring your awareness back to the present and gift yourself peace. When you do this repetitively, you create awareness of the space between stimulus and response. And in that momentary space you can return to your sacred center—the Medial place where Spirit can be heard, or experienced, no matter where you are. You do not need a meditation room or a delineated temple (although these things can be nice) to achieve this, as you are creating the temple and the meditation room within you. With practice you can return to your sacred inner space over and over again whether you find yourself out in the woods or on a bus. In other words, you can access oracular guidance no matter where you are or what you are doing.

In this sense, I often think of officers and firefighters who experience heightened intuition when they are in life-threatening situations. In these situations, they certainly do not have access to "ideal" conditions, yet they receive insight and guidance that often prove to be lifesaving. We can access helpful information if we learn to tune in and focus our awareness no matter our external environments, but it does take discipline.

I try to return to this practice repetitively throughout the day whether I find myself in the living room or outside, walking. I steady myself; I release the flood of thoughts that I am focused on, and I return to my center through stillness and silence. I have found that it takes me courage to return to a serene inner space when my thinking mind or the noise of the outside world states otherwise. Some days are simply better than others.

It takes courage to be still enough to drop into the sacred center of your heart. To stand in the middle point between here and there, the seen and unseen, the place where your higher knowing and Spiritual strength can be accessed. **It takes courage to commit to sitting in stillness and silence for at least 20 minutes a day.** In relation to this and as a gentle reminder, research states that the average person spends between one to two and a half hours scrolling through social media daily![2] It is amazing how many minutes we can gather if we begin to bring greater intentionality to our often-habituated actions.

Many of us also know what it feels like to get so completely sucked in to what we are viewing that the outside world ceases to "exist" for those moments. In a similar way, when we drop into stillness and silence, our external environment ceases momentarily. We intentionally focus our attention and awareness inward (no matter what is happening around us) to access higher consciousness. We can do this for one or two minutes at a time or even for a few hours if we choose to. Sacred insights can drop in during a 30-second pause—there really are no prescriptive timelines.

That said, with a bit of practice, you will hopefully come to discover firsthand that you can commune with the oracle within you. It does take time to develop this practice, and it is simply not an option for some, which is okay. Do your best to find stillness, but let it be every day if you can. Try to make it a priority. Most people know deep down that this is true, but at the same time they understandably may find it difficult to follow through with the day-to-day consistency that is required of them to be in communion with larger forces.

Sometimes, the ritual of entering into sacred dialogue is also mistaken as the important "thing" when it is simply there to drop us into a quiet contemplative zone. In most cases, the ritual is simply there to help us condition the small mind into stillness and serenity—to help us move from ego perspective to Spirit perspective. Although the candles and tea and serene view are nice, they are most certainly not necessary. When I work with my trainees, I often teach them how to drop into this zone without external markers of significance so that the skill is deeply imbedded within them, regardless of where they find themselves or as to what resources they have at their disposal.

So, close your eyes and plant your feet firmly where they are. Know in your heart of hearts that you are greater than any of your thoughts and emotions. You are greater than any past or future experiences. It is safe for you to sit in the silence and stillness wherever you are right now. It is safe for you to hear Spirit and witness the unseen. First for a few moments, then for a few minutes, and before you know it, as often as you need and as often as is required of you. You are worthy of moments of stillness and deep knowing.

In our mythic story with Fedot, we even saw that he had to journey into a cave at the end of the narrative to gain perspective—in his case, to find the elusive Shmat-Razum.

To become a skilled Medial, this ability to enter into sacred space must become part of you. You must be able to enter into your inner cave with ease. Once there in the safety of your inner sanctum, you may be met with ecstatic experiences, common sense (like Fedot), or oracular knowing. What you experience will likely depend on what you need. You may be visited by your past lineage (not just from this life), as well as from other nonphysical guides that are currently assisting you. You may discover a new way of seeing the same old thing, *which then changes what you see.* Or you may simply go into the cave thinking one thing and return with one less-heavy burden of mind and heart. The sacred cave is to be honored and respected for access to the Soulful and precognitive gifts it provides us with, gifts that arise spontaneously when we are open to receiving from a place that is not ego-driven.

Here we also discover that caves as symbols are incredibly prolific. They are deeply held images ingrained within our collective psyches, partly because our ancestors found them to be so life-preserving but also because of what they naturally and Instinctually evoke in us, which is often an instinct to harmonize with the very quietness and stillness which naturally permeates a cave. Even rock art found within caves often points to trancelike and higher states of consciousness through the images of spirals and constellations. It is like we go inward in order to go higher in consciousness, and caves as a collective image remind us of this ability. They are truly sacred spaces that reflect these qualities back to us. We can see this so clearly in the story and experience of a team of archaeologists and anthropologists who journeyed into the Rising Star cave system. The journey was filmed in a Netflix documentary called *Unknown: Cave of Bones.*

It is a groundbreaking adventure in which lead paleoanthropologist Lee Berger and his team discover the bones of our ancient ancestors, known as *Homo naledi*. Their findings show that they existed as far back as 240,000 to 300,000 years ago and that they ritualistically buried their dead. This may not sound like such a big deal now, but imagine living in ancient times, when your life depended on moving for survival (finding food, for example). Stopping to bury the dead in a cave then shows the importance of something more than just survival. In my opinion, it shows connection, love, and deeper ways of living and being. It shows a dimension of Spirituality that is archaic. In Berger's own words:

> These recent findings suggest intentional burials, the use of symbols, and meaning-making activities by *Homo naledi*. It seems an inevitable conclusion that in combination they indicate that this small-brained species of ancient human relatives was performing complex practices related to death. That would mean not only are humans not unique in the development of symbolic practices, but may not have even invented such behaviors.[3]

The documentary and research findings have caused a stir in academic circles, but what I found most interesting was the connection to symbols and Lee Berger's own personal journey through the experience. He entered the cave as a paleoanthropologist and exited a man in awe. It is important to note that as a world-renowned expert, he has spent a substantial portion of his life dedicated to his work—work that we then collectively benefit from. He and his team also braved a potentially life-threatening situation to descend into that cave to discover the ancient predecessors of the land for our greater collective understanding.

That said, I believe that he entered into a Spiritual initiation without perhaps intending for that to be the experience. By entering into that cave, he went through both a literal and intrapsychic rite of passage, where he was initiated. The initiation is marked in a few ways. Firstly, the cave as a physical structure initiates him. In the documentary you can see the incredibly tight chambers that finally lead to the expansive inner sanctum of the cave, called the Dinaledi chamber.[4] The cave design almost "drops" him into the lower parts of the structure once he has traveled quite a distance to get there. It is a literal physical descent that goes inward, and Berger even had to lose weight to be able to enter some of the smaller passages.

We know that in many wisdom traditions, and even in contemporary practices, fasting is essential for entering into sacred dialogue and/or higher states of consciousness. Comfort, the same way of doing things, is sacrificed in order to enter into Spiritual communion. Berger, in many ways, did this but perhaps for more pragmatic reasons rather than Spiritual ones—yet the action is done nonetheless. We often consciously mark rituals and initiations by both symbolically and physically preparing. This helps us to feel gravitas for what we are about to do, and it also helps us to come from a place of reverence and respect for a journey that may push us beyond our perceived limitations.

For our ancient predecessors the *naledi*, they, too, entered into the same cave and went through the labyrinth to bury their loved ones. They went "inward" to honor and protect what was sacred to them. In my mind's eye, I imagine them carrying their dead from the outside flatlands all the way into the cave and then to the final chamber, where they laid them to rest. And through those very actions, the place becomes even more sacred. It amazes me that this same cave has been used by two different species that go into the dark but for absolutely different reasons hundreds of thousands of years apart. Yet with our Medial Sight, we see that through the very same passages an initiation of the life-death-life cycle occurs for both species but in two fundamentally different time-space realities.

In Berger's experience, he found himself in what he described as an almost tomblike darkness, where he was met with absolute stillness. As with any initiation we rediscover our two old friends stillness and silence, the two keys to entering and exploring the sacred. Here we also see that an initiation of a Spiritual nature often requires becoming well acquainted with darkness of the unknown, as well as the stillness and the silence that naturally accompanies the journey. As Medial-minded people, we must consciously and willingly traverse spaces that are sacred in nature, but in order to do this, we must acknowledge that in many ways we must first surrender our previous "knowing" to gain new understanding.

Berger maneuvers through the dark passages and channels of the cave, and finally he reaches a natural column-like structure. On the structure there are visible symbols (a pictograph) carved into it. In this particular moment in the documentary, I felt absolute gratitude for his expert-level knowledge—he sees the symbols in the dark and recognizes them for what they are. He knows the difference between hand-carved symbols and patterns carved out by natural elements like water over time. Through his professional seeing and sensing, *our knowing is then expanded.* Isn't that amazing?

What happens to him next, though, is perhaps the real gift. He has what he describes as a hallucination (what I would describe as a Medial vision) in which he sees those very symbols move off the cave's column and glow in the ether around him. He explains the vision and likens it to a movie scene where a mathematician has a huge *aha* moment and the numbers spring off the whiteboard and start to glow in the three-dimensional reality around them. And in that instant, a new higher-order knowing and understanding arises. A crack in consciousness happens. Reality shifts, or perhaps his perception adjusted and he simply saw a truer reality. For those of you who have read my previous book, his experience kind of reminded me of what it is like to go through the hypnogogic passage of sleep consciously, where there is a spontaneous moment where the dream suddenly "pops up" all around you in your awareness in 3D. In either case, **it is like a set of locks finally opens up because the person has become the key.** We walk our consciousness through passageways of reality/dreaming and come out on the other side with a greater vision.

In response to his vision, Berger remarked, "This shouldn't have happened to a guy like me!"[5] But I'm so glad it did, and I'm so grateful he shared his findings with the world in such an open way. In many ways, how could that ancient and sacred site *not* initiate him? Perhaps he was exactly the right person to have that very Medial experience. Perhaps if it had been someone else and he had not been able to make these findings public, then we may have never known about this story, the symbols, and our predecessors. Maybe that decade-long journey was priming him for that very moment so that he could see *but also so that we could see too*. So that we as modern people could remember a deeper way of seeing everything that surrounds us.

Sacred spaces evoke just that—the sacred.

Our ancestors found certain spaces to be inherently special, and they most certainly used what they had around them, caves then being a natural opportunity. Nowadays, we travel to sacred places in an effort to return to our own sacredness, to remember the ways Spirit was woven into the very fiber of the ancient world. We only need to look to the land, the pyramids, Stonehenge, Easter Island, or the many ancient ruins in the watery depths to see and feel the mystery that exists all around us.

I will never forget my own experience of going into a small cave (more like a crevice) in a mountain on one of the Mediterranean islands. The space was so small that I couldn't stand up straight, and I am pretty short. So, I curled down low and entered into it, and that is when I discovered that other people had left little offerings in it—a lit candle, a picture of someone whom I imagine was loved, flowers from the field a few steps back. This tiny cave wasn't listed on any travel sites. It was simply one of those exquisite "finds" you can experience when you travel. I stumbled upon it because it was about a block away from one of the more popular stone-built and man-made places of worship on the island. Yet there it was—Nature's tiny and potent sacred offering—right around the corner from man's sacred temple.

In that small physical sacred space, I remembered that I was sacred too. That the land births us, as it does our mothers. And that the statement that "we come into the world alone and die alone" could not be more untrue. We are literally brought into the world by our mothers—we could not be more together if we tried. We are birthed through them as they are held by the earth. Then, when it is time, we return to our earthen mother, and the land rebirths us all once more. *Alone* is a symptom of disconnection to all that is—an epidemic of modern seeing and believing. We have never been alone. We are held by Spirit, the land, and those who physically and emotionally hold us—core realities that many people have long forgotten.

The sacred cave or the quiet hilltop, these things may yet come for you, a sacred pilgrimage into your own inner divinity mirrored back by the land, but until that time, all you need to do is look around the room you are currently in. Lift your eyes off these pages and bless every corner of the space you find yourself in, no matter if it is a cubicle or crucible. Make it sacred with your blessings; bridge the sacred with the mundane with your willingness to see. The sacred will speak to you *anywhere* if you are prepared to listen with an open heart.

We must return to seeing things in a Medial way, and by journeying to sacred places, we can remember another way of interacting with everything and everyone that exists around us.

We are so lucky that we have the ability to travel to caves and temples to reconnect with our sacredness and, by virtue of that journey, rediscover our Medial Natures. But we are even luckier that if we cannot physically travel, we can then simply drop into the sacred containers of our own consciousness. It is neither one nor the other, one prize path over the other. We are simply and fortuitously provided with both potentials, and it is up to us to allow ourselves to receive the gifts they both offer. In the same way, we walk through life, and then when we fall asleep, we walk through our dreams. Two paths—one you.

In a *beautiful* time-space spiral, we see that the *naledi* chose to enter the cave, where they then prepared their loved ones for their next passageway—the afterlife. Berger then went into the very same cave and physically enacted a passageway to expanded consciousness. He experienced what psychiatrist Carl Jung described as the unseen or the collective unconscious—the storehouse of all shared symbols and images. This is the lower world of the psyche, like the lower chamber of the Rising Star cave. For us, we simply chose to enter that same cave through the passage of storytelling, and we were initiated into symbolic remembrance—the starter language of the Medial Nature. One cave providing multiple journeys, depending on how we look at it and who is taking the journey in whatever time-space they find themselves existing. What a sacred space indeed.

At the end of the documentary, Berger and his team tell the audience how those very symbols that were found in the Dinaledi chamber had also been found in ancient sites all over the world, spanning a vast period of time. In essence, the *naledi* carved the symbol around 300 thousand years ago. Then the Neanderthals made the same symbol thousands of years later, and then our human ancestors did the same thing about 80 thousand years ago. The very same symbol that evoked a vision in Berger is now metaphorically etched into this book and perhaps your own psyche too.

The Medial journey, the Medial initiation, enacts itself in both worlds: the physical and the symbolic, bridging the unknown with the known both within ourselves and in the world at large. We see that we are part of both worlds like our predecessors were, too, and that one sacred space can be so valuable hundreds of thousands of years apart. Through consciously journeying into sacred spaces and getting quiet, we come to discover the deep and influential symbolic strata of the psyche. It is a wisdom that goes beyond logic, and it is experienced as embodied perceiving. It is the bedrock that holds the river, the very same symbolic substrata that can be consciously navigated by the Medial Nature.

Perhaps even then the image-maker of consciousness can be found in sacred spaces, and in those moments of greater awareness we have the opportunity to unify our dual awareness—if only for a moment. And in that split second of awakening we can see, *really see*, that we exist behind all stages of life, death, and rebirth. We see as our ancestors saw as they entered into those passageways to lay their dead to rest. That there is something far bigger than just physical life, and that life-death-life has always been the way. And now in response to this ancient cycle, I see mythologist Martin Shaw's words wrapped around Beiberikan—an ancient Siberian Wild Medial who is here with us also saying: "ENOUGH. *Enough.* Be kind to each other. Be kind. The dead have come back to life. *Be kind.*"[6]

The *naledi* stalk our stories, as Beiberikan circles our collective dream too, and they tell us what they see: the disconnect between now and then and the sacred nature and people we refuse to see.

Enough, be kind, they say.

As the dead may have to come back to life, and we may have to leave.

What then will we choose to see, I ask.

Wrong question, they say.

How should we choose to see?

With sacred sight in all time-space realities.

Choose to see life for all sentient things.

And how should we choose to speak?

Choose with kindness, they say, for the dead come back to life.

CHAPTER 10

LEARNING *TO* SEE *AND* HEAR *IN A* SACRED MANNER

Many Medials are psychic and have accurate dreams and visions—especially once they accept who they are. They are equally gifted in understanding the language of symbols and often come to actively learn about the power of the unconscious mind, as well as the unseen worlds to which they are highly attuned and sensitive to. In the previous chapter you saw how just one set of symbols found at the Rising Star cave has been found in multiple time-space realities and how the image still holds immense "charge" in the modern psyche. Symbols speak to us about ancient times and forgotten knowings that we often need to remember. They can tell us about the past, present, and future, as well as our connection to all of life. Medials understand that symbols are the stepping stones that connect intuition, psyche, and dreams, that through them we can track a larger pattern that they make. We can track our own greater awareness as well as the larger, ineffable cosmic mystery that we are all connected to.

In Australian Aboriginal culture, there are songlines or dreaming tracks that lead those who can still see and hear in a sacred manner to the original power places of the land and sky. They are symbolic tracks that intersect with physical reality, quite literally mapping the way forward for anyone who travels on the path or songline. These dreaming tracks are passed down through oral tradition, and when the older generations of Aboriginal people walked the land, they would sing the songs associated with each line that highlight the sacredness of the land and the creator beings associated with each place, as well as practical directions for food and water. Dreaming tracks link the sacred and mundane worlds together. They have a rich and complex meaning, especially given Australia's history. Wonderfully, they still exist and are pathways that can still be followed to this day if one can see and hear in a sacred manner.

As Aboriginal elder and educator Aunty Munya Andrews mentions, and as her teacher taught her: The Dreamtime isn't just for Aboriginal people—it is for everyone.[1] The Dreaming is for us all, as we are all naturally participating in its weaving, and at the same time we can acknowledge and respect the keepers of this wisdom. We can hold both realities in graceful equilibrium by holding respect for others, as well as ourselves, and by seeing the sacredness in all things. When we try to cut one another off from connecting to Spirit, we split off part of our own awareness and create more chaos and division as a result. The antidote, then, is to recognize the Spirit in all things, that symbolic tracks exist in multiple ways, and that through working with symbolic tracks we can begin to see one another and the entire fabric of life in a sacred manner.

Symbols offer us great guidance as both Spirit and psyche speak through them, showing us a path forward. This path speaks uniquely to each and every one of us while also connecting us to the larger collective—as it did for the Aboriginal people who followed the songlines/dreaming tracks.

Every night, when we sleep and dream, we step into the wonderful world of image and metaphor—our own symbolic track that leads us back home to Soul. When we ask the Universe for a sign and surrender our will, we see a dance between synchronistic events, symbols, and signs. We then recognize that when we receive these messages, we are right on track and about to hit our target in some way, *that we should keep going.* When we enter into this way of conscious living, we discover that we are in sacred partnership with Spirit, and we also learn about the depth of our very own sacredness. When you use a tarot or an oracle deck, you are leaning in to your Medial abilities to intuit what the symbols are saying about your current issue or question. You are using an inward track to intuit an outward path through an archaic medium of symbols.

With depth psychology, we discover that the psyche naturally produces symbols and that these are highly personalized. We learn that the psyche is loud and produces transformative symbols—especially when we need to resolve any tension that arises because of two internalized but conflicting points of view. This is why people will often have dreams of angels or messengers (like postal workers, delivery people, or the phone ringing) when they are emotionally or psychologically stuck in a stronghold between two opposing or conflicting elements. The dream then naturally arises within them and produces a third symbol. That is a transcendental track that helps mediate between the two opposing constructs. A Medial messenger or symbolic marker then spontaneously arrives and helps them to get out of the mess of dualistic thinking and feeling.

This is the track that you must hunt for if you feel fear, but also know that there is no other option but to step into the unknown. As the old, repetitive ways and symbols simply will not do, you must follow the symbols left by Spirit and trust that in the process you will be held in the depths of the unknown. **We must become master trackers of Spirit and our own sacred hearts.** If you are stuck or at an impasse, or when it is simply time, your psyche (leaning back to the ancient definition of the word here meaning *Soul*) will naturally evoke a symbol within you that will reconcile tension—and offer you a new perspective. *It will offer you an entirely new way of seeing—in other words, new awareness.*

New awareness is one of the greatest gifts we can receive because with it we can change reality. The unconscious (the unknown) motivators or elements and the conscious (the known) motivators or elements are brought into harmony and you feel the difference that that integration and new awareness make. In some ways this is similar to how when many of us were teenagers we thought we knew everything, and yet later we came to discover that we actually knew so little about so many things. Things were just so out of our awareness, or at least, I speak for myself here! Yet once you know what you know, you cannot unknow it. It is like what is seen cannot be unseen—there is new awareness, new sight. In other words, you grow as your awareness does.

Any internal tension of two colliding systems of understanding, knowing, or perceiving can be brought into balance by a mediator within the psyche. The psyche intrinsically knows when to instigate the mediator function and will do so to help you out of any binding tension that you cannot resolve through thinking. You can't have a higher perspective until it arises within you or something outside of you knocks you into a situation that brings you to a higher perspective. You can talk about it, meditate on it, journal about it, say affirmations hourly, but until it clicks in and is actually a lived experience, it is just a notion—an intellectual concept pointing you in the right direction. **So, our job, then, when working with symbols is to go from "thinking" about them to instead receiving wisdom directly from them.** Symbols are vitally alive within you, and in the outside world when they "come to life" we call it meaningful coincidence, synchronicity, or, to some people, a God-wink. (I love that divinity can wink at us; the question is, are you consciously winking back?) If a symbol can arise within you and then you see evidence of the same symbol in the world outside of you, what, then, is the connection? *Perhaps you and the unseen influencing the material world.*

Equally, one symbol can say many things, depending on who is doing the asking and what is happening for that person in their own lives. A good way to think about this is again through the medium of dreams. Imagine that both you and I have the exact same dream where we take a bite of a golden apple. But now imagine that in my waking life I am severely allergic to apples. So, what is this apple dream trying specifically to tell me? I would take the golden apple to mean that although something looks good and shiny on the outside, it hides something that would be poisonous to me. From the dream I would become aware and come to understand that a situation in my life was likely not all that it seemed to be. I would then activate my discernment to help me perceive what I was missing. On the other hand, say you had the very same dream, and you love apples in your waking life, then perhaps the dream is not warning you of anything; it is telling you to take that bite out of life. To enjoy the golden opportunity!

In myth we even find an enchanted apple that makes Snow White sleep for three hundred years! If her story somehow randomly appears in your life, perhaps it is time to pay attention to what enchants you into falling asleep to your own life. One symbol, three different meanings, depending on who is receiving it and what is taking place in the person's life at that specific moment. Ultimately, reading symbols is an ancient art, just as it is the Medial Woman's mother tongue.

During the course of writing the mythic initiation for this book, I had the following dream filled with many prolific images and symbols:

He arrives as a Medial Man, a guardian of thresholds, and he comes to tell me not to waste time in choosing. (If I could draw with even a slight modicum of talent or skill, I would etch his face into paper, although I imagine the image of him will stay with me for a very long time.) I find myself in the dream standing knee-deep in dark lagoon water. It is nighttime and I am aware of the fact that there are lampposts on the edge of the water's embankment. The light comforts me, but at the same time I feel worried that I cannot see what is in the water with me. I have a fleeting thought about alligators, but my thinking is interrupted when I realize that I am not alone in the water.

From a distance, I see a man standing waist-deep in the water, and he is holding a long stick. The stick stands vertically upright like a staff or cane and is half-submerged in water. He is a middle-aged man who has ash on his face, and he is trying to tell me something, but I cannot hear him from so far away. I motion toward him, but he is still speaking, and I feel like I am missing something, so I stand still and try to lip-read what he is saying. I realize he is saying: "Don't waste time choosing."

Once he sees that I've understood what he has said, he then takes a deep breath in and makes a triangle shape with his hands and then places them over his mouth. Then, from the depths of his being, he breathes smoke out toward me. It hits me from across the water and covers everything, and all I can see is smoke. Somehow in the dream I understand that through the smoke he has offered me cleansing and a blessing of protection.

As dreams do, the scene then shifts, and I now find myself standing outside an ancient amusement park that has multiple entrances that lead into different paths and rides. The park doesn't have modern equipment. Instead, it looks like it is built from rock and stone, just as if the Sphinx were a feature at a carnival ride. It's a juxtaposition image of a modern game set in old structures. At this point in the dream, I am standing with two people I know very well, and I am aware that we must choose a path quickly because I was told not to waste time choosing! I tell the one person who wants to go right that he should stay with us, but he wants to go. So, we let him go, but we know that he has chosen a more difficult path. We then decide to go left and enter into a massive space that has hundreds of artifacts framed on the walls. As I move through the huge space, I begin to become aware of the fact that things seem to be moving on the walls and floors.

I catch glimpses of movement, but I can't really make out what I am looking at, as the space is very poorly lit. Suddenly I realize that there are snakes everywhere, and I am so creeped out, but there is absolutely no turning back at this point. At the same time, I also instinctively know that if we stick to the middle of the path while not touching the railing, everything will be fine. We move through the entire space, and the ramps then start to take us upward when a strange old man appears behind me. I recognize him, but I can't hold on to anything, as the dream is moving very quickly. At one point I see that he is still behind us, but he is struggling to climb over a railing to be able to get out of the "ride." So, I turn around and help him over. I notice that he has a cane with him, which he then leans against the railing, and somehow it becomes part of the structure. Then, all of a sudden, he easily hops over the barrier, and we all find ourselves on the other side—outside, in the daylight.

Standing outside, I notice that there is a concession stand, and I know that I must give this old man a drink. I pick up a green smoothie and offer it to him, and as I do, I have the thought that perhaps the drink was intended for someone else. But I know better than not to offer it to him. He nods in appreciation, smiles at me, and then goes on his way. The dream then takes me and the other person into a new scene. We are now in a hotel, and we have to find the door that leads to the outside, and if we do that, we will have made it out of the game entirely. I find the glass door and turn back to see where my partner is. . . .

And in that moment, I wake up.

A MEDIAL WOMAN AND HER SYMBOLS: THE CROSSROAD LANGUAGE OF INTUITION AND DREAMS

There are many ways to make meaning of this dream, and perhaps you already have an idea of what that is. When we work with symbols and image, there is an intrinsic link to words and how they influence our reality. In many mystic traditions such as in Hinduism, Judaism, and Buddhism, we are taught that words have power. Not just metaphoric power, but *real power* to create and alter what we experience and see in our reality. That's why it is so important that with any intuitive readings or dreamwork, the intention is to read the symbols in such a way that a positive meaning is evoked for the person whose imagery is being worked with.

Even a dream or symbolic message of warning should be read in a way that is helpful as opposed to fearful. After all, these are mirror images of something within us that needs to be brought to light. The image is frightening but not settled in reality, so we are warned to be aware of where our intention is aimed. We are shown that there is still time to shift our energy and experience toward something better. In this way we are then incredibly lucky to have off-kilter dreams or intuitive messages that at first may seem strange but that help us immensely. In tarot imagery, there is a card that on the face of it looks horrible. The image is of a man lying face down with 10 swords in his back. The card shows us to be on the lookout for betrayal both out in the larger world and through our own actions. Seen in this way, the image is then immensely helpful, as we can use the information to shift the direction of things. *To take action in a different way.* It could also be a retroactive message where we are simply being told that what is done is done and that we can make amends toward ourselves and others for having chosen that path previously.

When we face the imagery, we then remove the "charge" linked to the images. We see our own inner projections and discover what message the symbols and images are trying to tell us. This is why even just writing down a dream or waking vision is helpful, because at the most basic level, the energy behind the imagery has at least been acknowledged. We take the images that evoke fear within us, and we return them to light by actively working with them.

Like many writers know, writing is often an initiation in itself, because you can only take people as far as you have traveled yourself. So, my dream arose from the depths to help me through the passageways of what was toward what will be. And it was absolutely no accident that I had this dream during the writing of the mythic portion of this book. The dream in many ways came to ask me whether I had the courage and commitment to make a wise choice, a question that I now mirror back to you—can you rely on your heart to illuminate the path forward? Can you trust your own connection to the Medial Nature—to be held and helped by the unseen—even if you must traverse in the dark for a while? Can you come to a place of confidence within yourself where you no longer fear the dark but begin to relish your dance with it?

When you work with any Medial Guide, you are in many ways consciously choosing to step into liminal thresholds. You are actively learning to traverse the in-between, and in this space you must actively let go of your comfort zone. But know this: When you walk toward the mystery, you walk away from constriction. Trust in the process of growth and expansion, as the in-between is the place where familiar patterns are interrupted and the realm of infinite possibility opens up.

It's a bit like when you were a kid and outgrew a pair of shoes, you'd get a new pair that fit. Hopefully you didn't have to cram your feet back into the wrong-size shoes, which would have left you hobbling forward on your path! In the in-between as adults, we must conscientiously strip ourselves of the items of identity that bind us. The shoes of well-trodden paths, beliefs, and knowings. We must walk barefoot in the vast mystery knowing that we can rely on our Medial Natures to track the path forward. While we are walking through any passage of initiation, we are at the same time metaphorically weaving into matter a pair of shoes that will fit the new version of ourselves. Our future self, who is patiently waiting for us on the other side of any personal initiation or collective time period of transformation.

So, whenever a crossroad appears in life, as it did in my dream, we are inherently met with a decision—which way should we go, and with that, which shoes are we willing to forgo? Often, we also tend to think that a crossroad means that we need to decide between two paths. But if you look closely at the symbol (X or +), you will notice that there are actually four pathways offered, not just two: the vertical above and below and the horizontal left and right. It is through our Medial Natures that we can traverse each and every direction as necessary. One life circumstance may also require that you traverse multiple paths to become adept at riding the wave of what is and what shall be. Loss is a great example of this, and so is leaping toward a brighter future.

What can one do here?

At the beginning, there is often nothing to do other than to sit with the discomfort. Eventually, we can move to acceptance, but it may take time. One has to allow what is polarized to voice or show its respective point of view. For example, you may intellectually want to do something, knowing that it would be good for you in the material world (a relationship or job), but emotionally there is resistance and fear stemming from something deeper within that is out of your awareness. Both your fear and your mind are equally speaking—each side as valuable as the other in this situation—but they are in opposition to one another. This is a naturally uncomfortable position to be in, and many of us often suffer when we are in this space. It's helpful to acknowledge this because denying the immensity of the situation just creates more tension. Yet in the discomfort of tension, we are actually being provided with an opportunity to grow, but we are required to step forward, having nothing other than our Medial Natures and instincts to rely on.

In this space it is also easy to become stuck if one does not make a decision as to which path to take. But really, feeling stuck is often just an invitation to become still. Stop running, slow down, and *listen*. Lean toward trusting, not overthinking. If you can turn to face what is happening, you will naturally have the opportunity for substantial growth and integration. When we don't face the tension, that is when we experience symptoms as a result of our avoidance, which can manifest themselves in a multitude of ways, such as anxiety, weepiness, anger, lethargy, or even depression.

This is when the unconscious mind begins to affect a great influence.

In this space it is then common to have vivid dreams or see images that evoke strong emotions. Often this is so one can open up to the higher perspective, waiting to come through, which will bring movement to whatever has become stagnant. In this Medial space of liminality, we go from needing or having to know toward *surrendering and relating* to what we are experiencing or being shown. We move toward a new transcendental and transformative path by trusting the symbols that appear on our path. Step by step, we trust the mystery to guide us away from feeling stuck, into the unknown, and then through to the other side. **These symbols alert us to the greater lucidity that we can experience in waking life, as they show us how to move past tension created by two opposing thoughts, beliefs, or emotions. They provide us with a new way of seeing, knowing, and perceiving.** In this way we can embrace pain and joy equally by discovering the higher potential behind both experiences.

In simple terms, one must relinquish control and step into the flow of life, where a new version of the self or situation can be regenerated and then rebirthed. Then one morning you wake up and suddenly you've gone from healing to healed, from stuck to new life, and from seeking the path to being on the path. You are quite literally on the other side of whatever "it" was because both release and integration have happened.

Let us now return to my dream to meet the Medial Guide who presented himself twice to me. We return so that I can show you how a Medial Guide will often show themselves to you if you are really committed to changing yourself or your life for the better. We also return so that you can see the symbolic thread between the language of intuition and the language of dreams.

Let's unpack this: I see a middle-aged man who is standing hip-deep in water. He has a stick (a staff) that is being held half in and half out of the water. He tells me not to waste time choosing. The dream continues, and then I meet an older man who has a cane, traversing the middle path that we are on. He needs help getting over a railing, which I extend to him, but somehow it turns out that he can actually get over the barrier with ease. I offer him a drink at the end of the dream.

Prior to my dream I had no conscious awareness of the fact that this dream figure represents a well-known West African, as well as Haitian, figure (or loa), known as Papa Legba. But since the dream was so intense, I woke up in the morning and researched what he looked like. That is how I discovered that he is a guardian of crossroads, a loa of stature. Papa Legba is known as someone who mediates between the Spirit world and the world of humans. He is a gatekeeper and is often depicted walking with a cane and dogs. It is also said that he is able to communicate in every single human language.

Here we see the many faces of the Medial archetype or Guide. A Medial Guide can and will present themselves to you in a multitude of ways. They are not fixed in image or form. Hekate (queen of the night) is another example of a Medial Guide— she is a Hellenistic guardian of the crossroads who equally is depicted with dogs in imagery. She, too, grants access to the thresholds between the seen and unseen. We see the thread between the Medial Nature and the way it can and will weave itself through different cultures and even modern dreams.

When we open ourselves up to receiving insight, we are then in touch with the core essence that can move between realms. This essence can show itself in many ways and through multiple faces, such as maiden-son/mother-father/crone-elder. In our mythic tale we even saw that Blue Dove represented the Medial Maiden, Baba Yaga the Wild Medial, and Kwa-Kwa, our old frog, was the Medial Crone. Interestingly, Hekate is often symbolically associated with frogs, too, and so we see a link to our old frog here, as well as in ancient Egyptian culture with the goddess Heqet, who is linked to frogs and is a Spiritual midwife/guardian). We see over and over again the same thread woven through different stories and stages of life, and with that experience of time, a granting of higher wisdom and knowing arises.

I believe that my dream presented itself to me in this specific way for a few reasons. Firstly, to show me how at a crossroad it is often best not to waste time, and secondly to show you, my dear reader, another good example of a masculine representation of a Medial guide. The dream also showed how the middle path (moderation between extremes) is often what brings safety and balance when we are faced with the depths of the unknown. (The Middle path or Middle Way is also a well-known Buddhist concept and so once again we see multiple layers of insight provided through just one dream). The Medial Nature shows us that there is life to be lived in the in-between because we are the living embodiment of awareness actively experiencing it. The dream also presented a transcendental and transformative third symbol—a hotel with doors leading to freedom. Whenever we find ourselves lost in the dark, not knowing what to do, we must remember that *our own awareness* can open us up to higher knowing. This is when our Medial Natures will show us the way forward—in my case Papa Legba led me to a hotel which would lead me out of the "game" and toward freedom. In that moment I woke up from the dream.

As someone who teaches others about the power of lucidity, I believe that we must "awaken" from the dream and recognize it for what it is. We must awaken from the dream of waking reality as well as our nighttime dreaming. I also don't mean "awakening from the dream" in a symbolic or poetic way. I mean it as an active state of awareness or consciousness—one that can lead to freedom. There are many schools of thought, both modern and ancient, that discuss this concept of awakening and attempt to explain the nature of our reality. (This type of lucidity and awareness is something you can read more about in my first book, *The Alchemy of Your Dreams,* should this interest you.)

Buddhists maintain that we are born to a cycle of rebirth (samsara), and that through lucidity we can escape the cycle by recognizing the in-between stage (bardo) that occurs after death. Freedom from illusion, or freedom from the "game," in my dream, also means recognizing when we are stuck in the illusions of the mind, and that we can indeed free ourselves by recognizing our true nature—the greater nonphysical aspects of ourselves. Just as a Medial Guide can traverse the seen and unseen worlds, so, too, can we if we remember who we truly are. There is no separation other than the separation we create with our minds, and the symbols we receive often remind us of this fact. We also see this when we experience meaningful synchronicity, as we are reminded that there is a larger picture at play. In other words, things aren't as fixed or as separate as they seem. And just as Deepak Chopra says, "Your mind is the knife that cuts the continuum of space and time into neat slices of linear experience."[2]

Won't you let it expand out toward your true nonphysical essence where you go beyond linear experience?

You can—it's just one thought away, as is your true nature.

When we directly experience the numinous or have a mystical encounter (like audibly hearing Spirit or meeting a Medial guide), it is awe-inspiring and terrifying all at the same time. Mythologist Joseph Campbell often referred to this experience as "mysterium tremendum et fascinans," expanding on a concept from theologian Rudolf Otto.[3] It describes the way that a real and direct experience with the numinous can be both tremendous and horrific because it decimates all your fixed notions of things, and at the same time it is utterly fascinating because it is of your own nature and being.

We can often forget how enormous a true shift in consciousness can be and feel. That higher awakening often comes at the cost of tremendous effort, familiarity, and releasing of identity. Yet when we consciously come to work with our Medial Natures, we discover a greater depth to our true nature. We *experientially* discover that we are nonphysical and physical at the same time, and that our nonphysical essence is the larger aspect of ourselves. Then our journey often becomes one of discovering the depths of how "big" and numinous that nonphysical part of us really is. There is so much more to discover.

A mindfulness teacher once taught me a practice in which you drop your name from your vocabulary and mind for a couple of weeks. The teaching is a simple one, but the practice not so much. When we drop our names, we are, in many ways, left with something larger than the identities that both help and bind us.

I am grateful that there are many ways for us to expand our perspectives. Just as Joseph Campbell expanded our perspective when he cloaked familiar words in Latin, *mysterium tremendum et fascinans*, helping us to drop into a state of curiosity. Here we are asked to look and listen to something familiar but from a new perspective. **While the meaning of the words remains the same, our sense toward them often changes, and with that both our perception and reality are free to be altered.**

This is the same thing about how we approach our true nature. We can become so accustomed to believing that reality and our identities are fixed that when we actually have a mystical experience (which expands what we believe our true natures to be), it can indeed be jarring. I once worked with a client who really wanted to develop their clairvoyant and mediumship abilities and so he held the intention day in and day out for weeks. Then one day he was standing alone in his kitchen when he turned around to "see" a deceased loved one. The experience both terrified and inspired him. Now when he "sees," he isn't so jarred, but at first it was quite shocking. **This is because one actually has to move from believing to experiencing, and sometimes it is simply easier to hover in the realm of believing than to actively allow reality to expand.**

Numinous experiences like he discovered can evoke greater insight, and in those moments of wonder we can truly recognize and expand our own awareness. We can see ourselves and the world with greater clarity. It is often in the everyday use of our words that we can easily forget the actual potency and meaning behind the words themselves. The word *Soul* has been tagged over 35 million times on just one social media platform as of writing this. There is absolutely nothing wrong with this—it's just to say that often in the mundane use of words, especially those connected to the unseen, it's easy to unintentionally nullify their meaning.

Medial, Medial, Medial can just as quickly become *pasta, pasta, pasta.*

Ancient languages force us to refocus, to really pay attention to the mystery that we are experiencing. So, whenever I feel stuck or just like the world is feeling all too familiar, I flip the mundane by finding new sounds and ways of seeing. I refocus my perspective by paying attention—by absolutely realigning my awareness with Medial sight. Day-to-day life can breed mundane seeing if you allow your attention to be numbed out with repetitive *thinking and knowing.* Yet our Medial Natures require us to see familiar things anew—to stay awake to the possibilities of expanded perception that can happen in everyday life. Our Medial Natures require us to stay awake to our own miraculous nature, to sit in stillness to hear and see with greater awareness, to wake up as beginners every single morning.

Think of it this way: It's like owning the *Mona Lisa* and putting her up on the wall. At first, you may experience awe and wonder every time you look up at her. But fast-forward a couple of years later—would you even bother to look? Probably not, because you've already seen her so many times. Maybe you'd think there is nothing new to be seen. Or maybe you wouldn't even think about it—it would just slowly happen as you became more accustomed to the picture being there. Yet with Medial Sight there is always something new to be seen and experienced. There is an internal knowing that says even an old image can show you something well beyond the static projection it portrays—*look closer*. Perhaps, then, one day you'd be walking past dear Mona and you'd notice that she winked right at you!

To be a Medial is to be one who is awakened to this larger part of themselves as well as someone who willingly and consciously enters into divine communion. There are many ways to enter into communion with the unseen. We can enter into divine communication through dreams, psychic sensing and knowing, by asking for a sign, meditation, stillness, through mediumship, and by using oracle cards. In fact, even the word *oracle* stems from the Latin word *orare*, which means to speak or to pray and to be in divine communication. In all cases what we are doing is simply getting into a bidirectional relationship and dialogue with higher consciousness (our own), as well as with Spirit.

In the original writings by Toni Wolff, a Medial Woman was someone who was in touch with her mediumistic abilities. She meant it as someone who could mediate between the unconscious and conscious aspects of the psyche, the realm of image and emotion, as well as liminal thresholds. In our times, most people understand the word *medium* to mean someone who can communicate with those who have crossed over, like deceased loved ones, family, friends, and even pets. It is also understood that although most mediums are psychic, not all psychics are mediums (we'll dive into this clarification later on). For now, it's simply important to note that in all these different definitions, it is likely the Medial function of the psyche that is being used. The word *Medial* encompasses both Toni's definition and our modern-day understanding of mediumship. **Because the Medial aspect of the psyche speaks to a wide spectrum of perceiving, it is both psychology and Spirit—just as you are both physical and nonphysical.** As such, I would like to further expand the definition of the word *Medial* to include the nuances of these differentiations. I do this in order to bring the Medial Guide into our times and to take our conversation even further.

A Medial is someone who can consciously and intentionally expand their perceptual abilities to bridge the unseen with the seen and in doing so become a conduit for the specific insight that they are focused on receiving. The Medial function within the psyche is what helps to bridge, connect, and mediate between two things. This can be done internally and externally. What differentiates the outcome, then, is where we initially and intentionally focus our attention before we start bridging the unseen with the seen. Equally, whatever implicit fears and resistance one holds will influence their ability to connect clearly in a Medial manner.

Perhaps in the future people will use the word *Medial* to encompass any form of nonverbal and/or nonphysical communication, sensing, and knowing. It is a large umbrella term and should be used to help liberate modern people from the ancient stigmas associated with "other" ways of sensing and seeing. *Charlatan, soothsayer, weird*—these words cut off life from the Medial Nature within. It is time to make these "other" ways of seeing and sensing normal. To be a Medial is to be someone absolutely grounded in the reality of this world while at the same time being able to expand their awareness out to include that which lies beyond. We have to normalize this "different" way of perceiving so that we can make a leap in our collective evolution as a species. I also wanted to ensure that the Medial archetype is understood to be an intrinsic aspect of the psyche—if you exist, you have the ability to connect to this aspect of your true nature.

It is not something that only gifted people can do, although when you exercise the skill set, it does indeed feel like a blessing. We all have this ability to connect, but like a muscle, it must be used and strengthened, otherwise it can weaken and atrophy. Some families pass down the belief that they can see in different ways, and others teach their children that only foolish people believe in these things.

We must reclaim the Medial ability as something totally natural and normal, and for you to grow, you must discover where you sit in relation to your own Medial abilities. This is often discovered through trial and error, persistence, and practice. This is also where you must come to rely on your Wild Instincts to discard any beliefs that your culture, family, or inner critic affirms that hampers your ability to perceive in a Medial manner. A Wild Medial simply knows better than to believe an old, limiting belief, whether it is handed down or self-enforced. Yet, to fully trust in the unseen and your connection to it, is helpful to understand the many ways that the Medial Nature can work. This is a wonderful learning space to be in where you get to discover and further develop your own intuitive and Medial abilities. It seems that there's always a greater depth to discover when we work with both higher consciousness and our own inner worlds.

CHAPTER 11

UNDERSTANDING YOUR OWN INTUITIVE ABILITIES

One of the most incredible things about language is that it can help us define and delineate large portions of information so that we can break things down into easy-to-understand notions. But one of the key features of the Medial Nature is that it is a fluid force—so the minute you delineate it into something concrete, you split it in order to define it. For our purposes it is helpful for us to categorize the Medial Nature into neat quadrants—but know that these are not fixed. This is so that you can test out where you stand in relation to your own intuitive abilities and Medial Nature. The more you develop your own connection to your Medial Nature and your own greater awareness, you will see how connected everything is. For example, synchronicity is a good example of how these worlds or quadrants intersect. But for now, let's look at these three quadrants:

1. Your inner world
2. The exterior world and other people (the objective world)
3. The nonphysical and the Spirit world

Now, which quadrant or world you are diving into will depend on where you find yourself in relation to your Medial Nature. You can move back and forth between these quadrants depending on what you personally need and what you are trying to accomplish. Remember, the Medial Nature is like the bridge you travel on to connect with the other side of the quadrant. Just like the mythic goddess Iris who traveled on a rainbow bridge, your Medial Nature is a functional mediator and bridge. It can help you to perceive white light in a range of colors—in other words, to perceive the things that exist but are not always so easy to see. Let's begin with the first quadrant, which is the connection to your Medial Nature in relation to your inner world.

As you've seen earlier in this book, the Medial Nature can connect you to your **inner world**. This is the quadrant Toni Wolff was mainly working with when she initially defined the Medial Woman back in the '50s. Again, she maintained that a Medial Woman was someone who could mediate between the unconscious and conscious aspects of the psyche, the realm of image and emotion, as well as liminal thresholds. We've seen how this is true. In this space the psyche will become very loud and send vivid messages to alert you when there is a need to reconcile any tension within you in order to help you transform. Throughout the course of this book, you have also seen how transcendental symbols can naturally arise to help mediate any tension caused by opposing belief systems which are internalized within you. In this quadrant, it is normal to receive spontaneous symbolic insights through dreams, waking visions, and meditation.

Here we can also learn to rely on our Medial Natures to guide us through any liminal thresholds; different cycles of life, death, and rebirth; and through the different stages of life. My dream of meeting Legba, a Medial Guardian, is a good example of how we can become internally held and guided through different stages of initiation. There are other stories that speak to themes of internal and collective transformation, like those of Hekate, Mother Night, and the Lady of Guadalupe.

In this quadrant we experience the mythic steps that require integration so that we can move forward positively in life. I shared the tale of Blue Dove and Fedot in the hope that you would see how your inner world can transform through integrating with your Ego Self, Medial Nature, and Wild Instinct. Your inner world transforms when you illuminate all the key players of your own psyche. This is the realm of introspection and greater self-awareness. Whenever a symbol or story evokes a strong sense of emotion within you, it is helpful to recognize that it is actually a key to unlocking greater insights of your own inner workings. Know that when you want to transform your life, it is wise to look at your inner world first and activate your Medial Nature at the same time. Journey inward to clean up what needs releasing, and then commune with the higher forces that are available so that you can move forward on your Soulful path. Now, moving along to the next quadrant, we see that **we can also use our Medial Natures when we connect with other people and the external world too.**

In the earlier chapters of this book, I shared the importance of trusting your Wild Instinct and intuition. I shared the story of violence prevention expert Gavin de Becker and linked it back to our mythic Wild Woman to really highlight this quadrant. This means that in this space you should use your Medial and Wild Nature to connect with nonphysical and physical cues given off by other people and real-world circumstances, like simply not walking down a specific street because you get the feeling that you shouldn't. Or when you think of someone out of the blue and later that day they text you. This quadrant deals with your external lived reality and the other people who pop up in it.

It is the realm of the collective and you intersecting together while navigating with the help and use of your Medial Nature, Instinctual Wild Nature, as well as your intellectual mind. It is triadic perception at its best. This quadrant is the realm of the collective and the individual intersecting together, and because of this we also saw how the past can be linked to the present through seeing with Medial sight. I shared the story of paleoanthropologist Lee Berger and his mystical experience in the Dinaledi chamber to highlight this. We saw how in that moment, space, time, and consciousness expanded. I also shared the example of the dreaming tracks that the Aboriginal people use to identify the power places of the land; this illuminates the connection of the ancient past and present moment as seen through the Medial eyes. In this quadrant you may discover that you can use your Medial and intuitive abilities for both your benefit and the benefit of others. Think of a tarot reader or psychic who offers readings; they, too, are working with symbols and images while using their Medial Sight to translate these messages to their clients.

Let us now move to the third quadrant, where we discover that **we can also use our Medial Natures to connect with the Spirit World and Nonphysical World** in an even greater way.

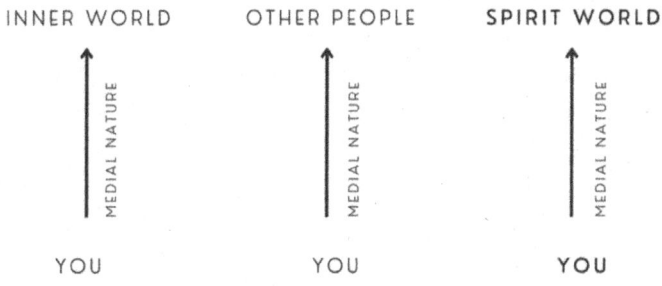

This quadrant deals with the unseen worlds in a tangible way, and it is through the everyday use of your own Medial Nature that you will come to experience this directly. In this quadrant, you can use your Medial Nature to actively connect with Spirit or nonphysical aspects of yourself, like the Soul. In relation to this quadrant, the word *Medial* really highlights the classic sense of the word, meaning *mediumistic* (i.e., mediumship). That is, you can choose to develop and use your Medial Nature to help others receive messages from the Spirit World, like deceased loved ones. Or you can simply use your connection for your own Spiritual and personal growth by connecting to the Soul aspects of yourself as well as by speaking with the Spirit team unique to you.

The Medial ability exists within all of us. It is a wide and vast function of the psyche. It can help us to relate better to our own inner drives, impulses, and beliefs. In other words, our inner worlds. It can also help us to connect to higher and intuitive consciousness. It can facilitate all these things, so it is important to realize that you naturally move between these quadrants as your life dictates. You may find that your inner world comes into hyper focus as a relationship develops or when a life change happens. At the same time, you may discover that you are guided by higher forces in the unseen realms that are supporting and helping you through any changes. It is a dance between you and this beautiful mystery that we call life. One foot here, one foot there.

Ultimately, awareness is what creates perception, and when you consciously begin to work with your Medial Nature, you will come to see how it naturally moves you to where you need to be. You come to heal from singular sight and lean in to a far more multidimensional way of viewing the world. It involves learning to deeply trust, over and over again, in forces so profound that our thinking minds must step aside.

Take a moment now to simply think back on any "strange" intuitive or mystical experiences that you've had over the course of your life.

Perhaps you can pick up insights about people you've just met but don't know exactly how you do that. That is using your Medial abilities in a naturally orientated way of extrasensory seeing and perceiving—in this case receiving psychic insights. Maybe you've had dreams of people who have crossed over and simply thought that it was wishful thinking at the time. Perhaps you can always tell where the empty parking space in a jam-packed lot will be. Or maybe you channel your own higher consciousness every time you create something. You know, that feeling of being one with a force that flows directly through you. **In all these cases, the Medial Nature is what facilitates a bridge, which arises within your very** own consciousness and helps to expand your awareness to perceive beyond what is right in front of you.

Over the course of my life, I have had varying attitudes toward my own Medial Nature. Perhaps you are the same and notice that sometimes you are so in tune and at other times this Soulful connection takes a back seat. Often those "backseat times" are actually when we need the connection most! Over a decade ago, when I still worked as a traditional psychologist in private practice, I actively hid my Medial abilities. One day, a corporate client came to see me. She booked the session because she had lost her mother and was struggling terribly with grief, which in turn was understandably affecting her work. This added even more pressure as she worked in a highly cutthroat environment that did not afford room for feelings. She was also not in a situation where she could easily just ditch her work and do something else (although she eventually did leave).

We made great strides together with traditional therapy. Around the third session together we were in a period of sitting in comfortable silence when I heard an audible voice say "peanut." The voice was not hers or mine. Anyone who is familiar with clairaudience or who has ever had a disembodied voice speak to them in a dream can liken this experience to that. Either way, at the time, it would have been highly inappropriate of me to say, "Does 'peanut' mean anything to you?" So, I left the information aside. Fast-forward to a session or two later and we were both sitting comfortably across from each another when I got the sense that someone was lovingly pushing against my shoulders. In that moment, she said, "I sometimes get the feeling that my mother visits me—her little peanut—and I feel so loved that it washes over me."

It was a powerful moment. Looking back on that time together I felt an enormous sense of love and expansiveness in that room. It was parental in the most positive sense—like a guardian stood there with the two of us. I've had many psychic and mediumistic experiences over the course of my life, so although this kind of information was not new to me, it was a real indicator that I needed to step out of the confines of the work I thought I needed to be doing. Now I run groups for people all over the world where we actively connect to Spirit and those who have crossed over. That experience also showed me that Spirit will come through for those who often need it most regardless of how we see fit. There is a much larger picture at play than simplistic and dualistic thinking, and Spirit will move worlds if need be to get through to us.

Peanut's mother comforted both of us that day. We felt her even if we didn't see her. At the time I was dealing with my own dualistic thinking (hello, tension of opposites!) where I could not reconcile my identity of being both a psychologist and a Medial Woman. This was also before the social media boom, so it wasn't as easy to find community back then. But looking back now, I know better than to believe that excuse. Whether social media existed or not, I wasted time hiding when I should have been standing as a beacon, and other Medials simply would have found me. Either way, I can now say with confidence that I am open to the truth of who I am, and I wish the same for you too.

No matter where you stand in relation to your own Medial Nature, know that you can rekindle the connection with ease if you begin to make it a priority in your life. Why not take a moment now to reflect on how you have been using your Medial Nature so far? Do you find it most comfortable to work with your inner world? How about directly communing with Spirit or picking up on psychic hits when you are out walking? Or do you lean in to your instinct when a situation really calls for it? There are no right or wrong answers here. There is simply a way of moving through the world with greater ease and connection.

Both the psyche and Spirit speak to us even when we are not ready to listen. Yet the true joy comes when we begin to actively listen. Now, in order for you to enter into a mutual dialogue with Spirit and the nonphysical, you must be able to both activate a strong Medial bridge as well as your own clair-abilities. The "clairs" stand for a grouping of perceptual abilities known as clairvoyance (clear seeing), clairaudience (clear hearing), clairsentience (a clear sense or feeling), and claircognizance (a clear knowing). These clairs are part of how we come to perceive the messages, symbols, and insights that we receive from Spirit via our Medial Natures.

Your Medial Nature is like your ability to turn a tap on and off. The water that flows through the tap is the guidance you receive from Spirit. The way that you then interact with the water is through your clair-abilities. In essence, you turn the tap on, water flows through, and then you are free to interact with the water through your senses, like through feeling the water, hearing the water, and seeing it. So, the greater your ability to turn that tap on and off at will, the greater the flow or connection between you and Spirit is. Then the more heightened that your clair-senses are, the greater your ability to understand the messages that are being transmitted to you.

Let's take a journey in visualization to help conceptualize what these clairs look like. Imagine that you are standing outside next to a big and beautiful magnolia tree. Picture interacting with the tree with your physical senses: sound, smell, touch, sight, even taste. At first you'd see the tree and perhaps hear its leaves rustling in the wind. You could touch the trunk and feel the bark against your fingers. You'd then notice the fragrant smell of the blooming flowers. You could even lick a leaf! Through the different use of your physical senses, you would discover all sorts of information and clues about the tree. Now, say that someone blindfolds you and takes you to the tree. Your sight would be diminished, so your other senses would naturally heighten. In other words, you would adapt.

Now just imagine that Spirit or your higher self sends you an image of a magnolia tree (clairvoyance). Or you suddenly think of a magnolia tree every time you are interacting with a particular person (claircognizance). Or you hear an inner voice whisper "magnolia" in one of your meditations (clairaudience). You are using your intuitive senses, as they mimic physical senses, to translate the messages sent by Spirit. **Ultimately this is a spectrum of perceiving that increases as you open up your awareness and develop your Medial Nature. If your Medial bridge to Spirit is closed, then it is very hard to perceive messages from Spirit through your clair-senses.** Here's an infographic to help you visualize how this all begins to work together.

Once again we split the clair-abilities into categories for ease of understanding, but they definitely can, and do, work together, just like how your physical senses work together in helping you to fully perceive a magnolia tree.

Now, have you ever watched a show with a psychic medium?

They'll often say something like "I'm wanting to come to this side of the room. I'm hearing the name *Maude*" or "I'm seeing the letter *M* and a magnolia tree" and "I'm getting the sense that she was a larger-than-life personality." Just through those few sentences we can see the Medial Nature at play in relation to the clairs. In this case clairaudience (hearing the name *Maude*), clairvoyance (seeing the letter *M* and the tree), and clairsentience (sensing a larger-than-life person).

Depending on your own life experience and natural comfort level of perceiving you will generally tend toward one of these clairs. Let's return now to our image of a tap being turned on with a steady flow of water streaming through. The water flows every time you sleep or do any form of introspective personal development work. Here the guidance is focused on your inner world and current lived reality. Then you learn to turn the tap on in waking life and as a result you begin to receive a stream of information in the form of psychic knowing. Then you lose all fear and turn the tap open even more fully, and the result is now that you can connect with Spirit in a mediumistic manner. Finally, turn the tap all the way on; you've now become a clear channel. In this metaphor the water is always available, guidance is always available, one simply needs to learn how to turn the tap on and off. You can work to enhance whatever comes naturally to you, and then later develop the others if you'd like to.

BEGINNING YOUR PRACTICE

We'll now explore these clair-abilities in the range of psychic, mediumistic, and inner-world exploration. For each ability, I'll also provide an exercise so you can put what you've learned into practice.

If you feel disconnected from Spirit and your own abilities right now, please know that you can rekindle your connection with practice. As with forming any new habit, you should commit to doing the practice regardless of how motivated you feel. It's helpful to start off with a manageable commitment that you do on a specific day at the same time. For example, you could initially commit to doing these exercises at least once a week, like on Sundays at 6 p.m. for 30 minutes to an hour, when you won't be disturbed. A lot of the busy people whom I work with do one of these exercises every day when they are in the shower. Even five minutes is better than no practice, so fit these practices into your life in a way that works well for you.

Not only is this a helpful way to make your intuitive practice a routine, but it also sends out a message to Spirit that you are serious about your commitment to becoming more receptive. In other words, you are saying to Spirit, "Hey, I'm here, I'm ready and willing." The more room that you create in your life to develop your intuitive and Medial Nature the more likely you are to experience it. I know from my own experiences that you can become abundantly intuitive simply because you decide to be. Just keep at it!

Another very helpful practice to do is to simply buy a journal in which you write down every single intuitive or significant message from Spirit that you receive. Date the entries and mark down exactly how you were communicated with. Use this journal only for this type of information. When you have noted down quite a few experiences, you should then be able to see your own body of symbols and how Spirit communicates with you specifically. You should then be able to recognize which clair-senses you use most. A journal is also very helpful to have as a reference point if you ever fall into doubt or a dry spell where you feel disconnected from Spirit or your Instinctual Nature. You can then look back and see how many intuitive hits were accurate, and equally by reading these experiences, you may unblock whatever resistance may be getting in the way.

CLAIRSENTIENCE ON A PSYCHIC LEVEL

Clairsentience refers to a clear feeling or sense of knowing. Have you ever gotten the feeling that you were about to receive an e-mail from someone you'd been waiting to hear from, and then it comes through almost immediately after? That is clairsentience. Here's another example: I'm with my friend, standing in line at a coffee shop, when a couple I had recently just met decided to stop by and say hi. In that moment, I remembered the wife's name but not her husband's name, so I introduced my friend, hoping that he would say his name. He didn't. We all spoke for a while and then they left. Straight after, my friend turned around to me and said, "He feels like a Ben." I agreed, and then we just got to chatting about other things. Later that night, I went home and asked my husband what his name was, and lo and behold, his name is in fact Ben.

Clairsentience is often experienced as a feeling or a sense that comes through, just like what my friend experienced. On a psychic level it is when you directly pick up on information from the people or places around you. You are not receiving the information—say, the name Ben—from the person's late father, which would then fall into the category of mediumship.

Here's another example of clairsentience in action. Several years ago, I was invited to a podcast to discuss my first book. The host was a wonderful woman who shared that she often had a repetitive dream that centered around her losing all her teeth. She then asked if this common tooth dream really just signified anxiety, as so many articles and interpretation sites suggested. As she was speaking, I got the clear sense that her dream actually had to do with how well she was nurturing herself in connection to food, because I felt a hunger pang although I had just eaten. I then told her what I thought, and she shared that she mainly had the dream while she was battling with her experience of anorexia. As you can see, following your clear inner knowing even if it seems contrary to what the person is saying can lead to wonderful breakthroughs and greater connection.

In many ways we are also working with clairsentience in the psychic category when we discuss the Wild Instinct and its link to intuition. Just think about that example of our Wild

Baba Yaga standing on a street when she sensed that something felt "off," like someone wanting to steal her handbag. Because her Wild Instincts are turned on and alert, she would pick up on the bystander's intention and body language and act as necessary. Like the story told us:

She would absolutely turn around and stare them down before they even had a chance to get close to her, and in the glint of her eye, they would recognize a warning that told them she was feral to the bone should they dare come closer. They would recognize that they were dealing with an Old Wolf whose hairs were standing up on the back of her neck, alerting her to danger, and that perhaps it was they who should be concerned and not she.

Again, if your clairsentient abilities kick in and tell you, "Hey, there is something more than you can see here—pay attention!" then pay attention! That said, many people have experienced clairsentience and often simply dismiss it. Have you ever gotten the feeling or sense that someone was staring at you, only to turn around and see that you were correct? Research from biologist and author Rupert Sheldrake, Ph.D., shows that not only do people feel when they are being stared at, but they know the direction the stare is coming from.[1] In my opinion, this is another great example of clairsentience in action. Through our senses we are alerted to information about the environment—we get a clear knowing of something. In this case, that someone is staring at us, and we "feel" that even if they are far off in the distance.

"Don't turn down this street." "The energy feels off." "The house has a sad feeling to it even though it looks pretty." "They feel pissed off even though they are smiling." Here we pick up on intricate cues from both the physical and nonphysical environments, and we feel them as a clear knowing—a gut instinct, goose bumps, a visceral yes or no. As a result of this, clairsentients need to learn to discern what emotions or feelings are their own as opposed to what comes from the environment or people around them. In many ways, clairsentients who practice on a psychic level are like sponges who can absorb information and patterns from the places and people they interact with. As a result, they need to know when to "absorb" (a better word here is *observe*) and when to switch off their skill set so that they can move through life without feeling overwhelmed by people and places. In Chapter 14, I share practices that can help you to develop healthy boundaries in relation to your own medial nature and intuitive abilities.

CLAIRSENTIENCE ON A MEDIUMSHIP LEVEL

Here is the generally agreed upon differentiation between being a psychic versus being a medium. Psychics tend to pick up on information through energy, people, or environments, whereas mediums receive their information from nonphysical beings, such as departed loved ones or guides. Both psychics and mediums are also able to receive information through their own larger nonphysical source—that is, their own Soul self or higher self. Generally speaking, mediums also have psychic abilities, while psychics are not necessarily able to communicate with other realms. In my opinion these categories are helpful but only to a point. If your Medial Nature is turned on, you have the capacity to both be psychic and access your mediumistic abilities, but for the sake of ease of understanding, let's continue in this way. This full spectrum of awareness is something I teach my students about, and most of them come to understand that this is a skill set that can be learned.

When a medium leans toward the skill set of clairsentience, they tend to sense and feel the departed. In my own experience, it is like both our energy field match in frequency so information can be shared. Many mediums will often describe this experience as both their energy fields merging or having their "auras" merge. For example, the deceased person's mannerisms and energy are all felt and sensed by the medium, and they may then express these mannerisms to the client. Or they may feel impact or heat in specific areas of their bodies. For example, my chest feels heavy and I feel like I am struggling to breathe. The medium then relays this information to the family and it turns out that the deceased died of lung cancer, for example. Clairsentience on a mediumship level is experienced through the body and also as a sense: "I get the sense that he was very boisterous."

CLAIRSENTIENCE ON AN INNER-WORLD LEVEL

There have been many cases of people worldwide who have dreamed of natural disasters before they happened. I believe that because clairsentients are often highly empathetic and sensitive in nature, this may inherently make them more likely to have experiences connected to the collective. To my awareness there is no data around this, but it would make for a very interesting research study! A woman who joined a workshop and shared that she would often have these kinds of prophetic dreams. On waking she would often feel very helpless, because how was she to stop a tidal wave or earthquake? She then shared that she now works with this information by praying for the collective and the people affected and has set up donation circles. As such, her energy is transmuted into healing action. Oneness is our true nature, and some people deeply feel this as embodied empathy in the form of clairsentience.

EXERCISE: EXPLORING INTUITIVE FEELING (CLAIRSENTIENCE)

In order to enhance your own clairsentient abilities, you can practice the following exercise. Find a time and space in which you will not be disturbed. First relax your body, and then begin to bring awareness to how you feel in your body (where does it begin and end? Sense the energy of your own body) for at least 15 minutes a day for a month. Do this practice when you are alone, as you are learning to sense your own energy while also bringing awareness to any areas within your own energy system that may be blocked or too open. You are doing this so that you create a baseline knowing of feeling and sensing within your body.

Once you have done this practice a couple of times, then go to a place where there are people, like a mall or a coffee shop. Sit somewhere and see if you expand your intuitive sense of feeling. Focus on recognizing the difference between how you normally feel and the things that you are picking up about people who you interact with. Did your breathing become different as someone walked past? How did your legs feel? Any sudden pains or weird feelings? Those things are your clairsentient abilities kicking in. Then when you feel that you have a good handle on this, invite over a group of friends that you trust. Tell them what you are intuitively picking up on, and then ask them to confirm whether your intuitive hits were correct. This will help you to see whether your clairsentient hits are accurate or if you need to practice more.

CLAIRCOGNIZANCE ON A PSYCHIC LEVEL

Claircognizance is the ability to clearly know something without having prior knowledge on the matter. You simply get a clear knowing of something that previously was obfuscated from your awareness, and it happens in an instant. You might walk into a shop and then just "know" that the shop assistant whom you've never met before is pregnant but not showing, for example. In the psychic category, you are once again picking up information from the people and places around you. You will receive insights and knowledge that is pertinent to what and who you are interacting with, and through claircognizance you receive it in a flash.

CLAIRCOGNIZANCE ON A MEDIUMSHIP LEVEL

A medium gets a clear knowing of something because the deceased relays this information to them. Often this is experienced as a block of nonverbal information that simply comes through, just like the way you would download a file to your computer. The medium will then turn to the client and say, for example, "John, the documents are in the cupboard with the elephants carved into the wood." What was unknown simply becomes known.

CLAIRCOGNIZANCE ON AN INNER-WORLD LEVEL

Many people experience claircognizant moments when they are standing in the shower or running. It's like an instant download that shifts your inner world. This often happens spontaneously and when one is alone. An example of this could be someone who has struggled to forgive a family member, and then suddenly "out of the blue" they know it is time to forgive them. Equally, have you ever woken up from a dream or sleep with a clear knowing as to what to do? This is claircognizance as it relates to you and your own inner world. When you sleep and dream you are experiencing the height of your own inner world and the nonphysical. Scientifically speaking, the liminal passages between sleep and wakefulness known as the *hypnopompic* state. In this state, it is very common to have "aha" moments where what was once unclear becomes crystalline and hyper-clear. In many ways that liminal passage can act as a portal to claircognizant awareness. In this space, you can receive information that can assist you, and people often wake up with a clear knowing of exactly what they need to do.

Anita Moorjani, author of *Dying to Be Me* and someone who had a near-death experience, also describes how the deceased can send us thoughts.[2] This can happen again through dreams and in waking life. Here we see claircognizance in the mediumship category as it relates to our own inner worlds. You have a higher order thought, like to invest in a specific stock. Did you think those thoughts, or were they sent to you? Definitely food for thought! This is where you must learn to trust your own abilities and your own Medial link to the nonphysical as it relates to you and your own life experiences. Again, claircognizance is the experience of clear knowing, as it relates to you and others.

EXERCISE: EXPLORING INTUITIVE KNOWING (CLAIRCOGNIZANCE)

This category is probably the hardest to work with if you've never experienced it, as the guidance comes through almost instantaneously and completely. The best recommendation that I have to develop this skill is to ask someone whom you trust to write two letters with a short made-up story with key symbols and images. Then ask them to mail the letters to you. Obviously, your friend shouldn't tell you what the contents of the letters are. When they arrive in the mail, try to intuit what each letter is about before you open them. Did you get a clear knowing as you picked up the envelope? Or did you see an image? This exercise may also help you to develop trusting your initial instinct, or clear knowing, when you touch or interact with objects. Alternatively, if you can't do that exercise, then next time you find yourself in a parking lot, try to see if you can intuit where the next open parking space is. Ultimately, you may find that you are more comfortable with one specific form of your intuition. Honor what comes easily to you and develop that skill set fully before you move on to the others. You don't need to be all things. You can just be claircognizant. The main point is that you are enhancing your ability to receive guidance from Spirit through your Medial and intuitive facilities. And remember that Spirit will always get your attention in way that you find easiest to accept!

CLAIRAUDIENCE ON A PSYCHIC LEVEL

Clairaudience refers to clear hearing. In this category you hear an inner voice that relays information to you. Say you hang out with a friend or partner quite a bit, and all of a sudden you hear "Let's get takeout for dinner." So, you say, "Takeout sounds great," and then they say, "How did you know that's what I wanted to do?"

Here's another example: I once had a strange clairaudient experience traveling on a plane that was headed to Utah. As everyone was boarding, I noticed a young man walking down the aisle, motioning to where I was sitting. All of a sudden I heard an inner voice say "serial killer." Needless to say, it was quite off-putting, even more so when he sat right next to me on an absolutely full plane. It turned out that his father was a criminal psychologist whose work centered around assessing serial killers. He told me that he had been away for over a year and was simply very excited to be going to visit his dad. In other words, he was broadcasting his energy quite loudly on the plane and I picked up on it. Again, this example shows the importance of knowing when and how to open and close your Medial and psychic channels of receptivity. Clearly it is not always helpful to be open and picking up on psychic information in crowded places like a jam-packed plane!

CLAIRAUDIENCE ON A MEDIUMSHIP LEVEL

This is when a medium hears the departed or their nonphysical guides. When I was in my 20s, I went to a workshop on how to work with guides. The facilitator, a psychic medium, told us that connecting with our guides is just like tuning in to a radio station: You should literally move your head back and forth until you find the frequency. I will never forget how funny it was to look around the room and see a whole group of us bobbing our heads up and down with the great hope of tuning in to our guide frequency. Spoiler alert: Not one of us did in that moment, although many of us later did!

I share this with you so that you can see that this journey can be one of joy, playfulness, and open-hearted learning. We all have our own ways of getting in the "zone." If one way doesn't work out on the first try, keep going. If it still then doesn't work after giving it a very good effort, then move on to something else. There are many, many, pathways to Spirit, and you will find the ones that best suit you! Personally, my clairaudient abilities are heightened when I take long walks alone. Something about the physical movement is enough to occupy my thinking mind and senses, and in doing so, it opens up my clairaudient channel. I often experience the same thing when I fold laundry—there is something about the repetitive and soothing (*I know!*) action that just drops me into the zone. So, the next time you are doing some repetitive task, try to focus on just being open and receptive. Relaxing the mind while remaining softly alert to the action you are doing may very well just open up your own clairaudient abilities.

CLAIRAUDIENCE ON AN INNER-WORLD LEVEL

Now, this category is quite hard to define for most people. But if we think about it, many of us can identify with the voice of our inner critic. If you pay attention to it, you know it has a certain way about it—it is mostly negative and berating. In this way you can single it out and learn to work with the voice or simply ignore it. Well, in a way, being clairaudient is simply being able to hear the voice of your higher self or your Soul voice. The Soul voice is loving, clear, and insightful. There is a certain resonance to it. In this sense, becoming clairaudient is then simply learning to single out the Soul voice. And evidently by paying extra attention to the Soul voice, the Medial Nature also becomes well developed, which in turn then makes it even easier to hear Spirit.

In my opinion, if you can point out the voice of your inner critic, then you likely have the innate ability to discern your Soul's voice. Just start to *really* pay attention every time you hear that voice (the voice that helps you out), and you will start to hear it more. The Soul voice is always there, speaking to you. It exists whether you listen to it or not. The frequency of it is ever likely; you simply need to notice it more by shifting your attention toward it. Decide to hear the Soul and you will, just like when you are deciding to buy a car, and then you suddenly notice it everywhere. (By the way, for those critics, I do not believe this is a cognitive bias or the frequency illusion—test this out for yourself and question the nature of reality more than what is taught).

Listen to your Soul's voice, and you will then see signs and communications everywhere. You may discover firsthand how messages begin to materialize in your physical reality. Your attention has power, and a conscious shift in perception can help to open up both your Medial channel and clairaudient abilities. At first, you may hear your Soul voice in dreams and later you may begin to hear it in your waking life as you go about your day. It is once again a spectrum of perceiving and connecting that can happen while you are both awake and asleep.

CLAIRVOYANCE ON A PSYCHIC LEVEL

In this category you may see images or symbols that pop up in your mind's eye in relation to the people or places that you are interacting with. You may also see a full scenario play out in your mind's eye just like you are watching a snippet of a movie. A client of mine once told me about an experience she had as she was about to do her driving test to get her license. In her mind's eye, she saw a scene in which she fell face-first trying to run to the car because it was raining. At the time, she ignored what she saw and did indeed fall. Luckily, though, she got her license and also received the gift of reconnecting to her inner sight from that experience.

CLAIRVOYANCE ON THE MEDIUMSHIP LEVEL

Mediums receive images and symbols directly from the deceased that relay information and guidance. Some mediums can also see the deceased just as they would a living person. When I was younger I could see those who had passed, but like many children I "grew out" of this stage. It has taken a good amount of practice to reopen this channel of awareness, and I still lean toward receiving information audibly rather than visually. That said, clairvoyance is centered around imagery as the main way of receiving and perceiving information. This means that a medium may see symbolic images and/or the deceased. For example, a medium may be with a client and they then get two images—those of briefcase and a car. Then from these images they would know that the deceased died in a car accident on the way to work.

Mediums work with symbols and imagery in a way that many dream analysts do: We build up a body of symbols that mean specific things to us. We also work with collective symbols. For example, whenever I "see" a lemon, I know that it means that a relationship has soured. For another person, a lemon may represent the season of summer. Spirit knows exactly how to speak to you specifically, and they will use images and symbols in a way that will make sense to you. Like in a game of Pictionary, your partner (Spirit, in this case) wants you to get the right answer. The more you play with your partner, the easier it becomes to understand each other. Spirit is waiting for you to start playing!

CLAIRVOYANCE ON AN INNER-WORLD LEVEL

On an inner-world level, this means clearly seeing what naturally arises in meditation and nighttime dreams and understanding this as a form of insight that has nothing to do with physical sight. After all, in all these cases, your eyes are usually closed—so what are you really seeing? You are perceiving the state of your inner world and, in my opinion, alternative timelines, if you learn to focus your attention enough. Precognitive dreams and psychic visions are good examples in this category. You experience a dream or vision where an event happens, and then later it comes true in waking reality. The event could be something solely focused on your life, or it could be about the collective. It is helpful to note here that although we've gone through all these clair-abilities on different levels (that is, psychic or mediumistic/inner and outer worlds), they are all connected. Our inner worlds and outer worlds are connected just as we as individuals are all linked to the larger collective. You, me, we—we are all connected to one another and the other side. Equally, the clair range is not static. You may discover that you are able to move between different clair-abilities depending on what you are doing and where you find yourself.

Just as you naturally adapt and use your different physical senses in waking life, you have the ability to change and shift between the clair senses. Spirit and the higher nonphysical aspects of you will also adapt and use whichever channel is most available to them. So, if you've been working at developing your clairvoyant abilities, then they are really going to meet you halfway and send you guidance in the form of images and symbols.

Now, let's say that you ignore all the messages you experience. Why, then, do you think of a donkey every time you see that specific co-worker? Donkeys—how ridiculous! What you didn't realize is that your co-worker's child passed away and that they loved a particular stuffed animal—a donkey. Well, then, Spirit will try to get your attention in another way—so you then hear a soft whisper that says to go ask that co-worker if they are doing okay. But you don't. So that night you go to sleep, only to hear a loud booming voice in a dream that tells you to "speak to them." But you wake up and dismiss your dreams as day residue.

Okay, now Spirit really has to pull out all the stops, so they send you a synchronistic sign that you cannot ignore—or can you? You see a donkey on the side of a truck as you walk into the building you work in. Perhaps in this situation there is only one true donkey, and that is the inability to pay attention to Spirit. I have been there more times than I care to recount. And as the old adage says, when we know better, we do better—or in this case, we should do better.

For the most part, it tends to take a lot of repetition for most people to accept that the messages that they are receiving from Spirit are actually real. This is why synchronicity, meaningful repetition, and coincidence are so important, because they often force us to pay attention. We often make our higher selves and Spirit work very hard to get our attention. We tend to need big, bold messages so obvious in nature but totally unanticipated to believe that we are being communicated with. Yet we are!

We experience this communication through our Medial Natures and clair-senses. The clairs function on a spectrum of perceiving, just as our physical senses are varied. Now, if you brave it and focus on developing the Medial bridge further, then you can move from being a bystander, where communication happens spontaneously, to becoming an active participant in dialogue with Spirit. You're ready, if you're not already doing this, believe in yourself!

EXERCISE: EXPLORING INTUITIVE SEEING (CLAIRVOYANCE)

Begin this clairvoyance practice by setting a personal intention. An intention is a heartfelt thought that you put a lot of consideration and energy into. It's also a whispered declaration that Spirit can receive. It could be a hope that you have for your intuitive practice or simply for your life. Once you've set your intention, find a comfortable seated position. Then close your eyes and place one hand over your navel and the other on your third eye (the point on your forehead between your eyebrows).

Take a few deep, nourishing breaths and say the following words: "It is safe for me to explore my clairvoyant abilities. I am now ready to see intuitively for the highest good of all. I am fully willing to allow my intuition to blossom now." Then imagine that you are sitting alone in a very comfortable and welcoming movie theater. The projector screen in front of you is blank. It is an active representation of your intuition, and it is going to show you a selection of images that will be relevant for you. Sit and watch the screen for as long as you need. (If the screen remains blank, simply practice the exercise daily until you begin to see images. Also, some people never see images—something known as aphantasia—and that's okay. There are many pathways to receiving higher-order information.) When you are ready, bring your attention back to the present moment and write down what you witnessed. Again, it's helpful to note your intuitive experiences, because as time goes by, you will begin to notice how much of what you have intuitively seen comes true and/or is accurate.

THE CLAIRS VERSUS SIGNS FROM SPIRIT

As you've also seen, you can receive signs from Spirit in the form of synchronicity. For example, you turn on the radio and hear the lyrics of a song that helps you solve a problem that you are struggling with. Or you walk past a building and see a message in the form of a poster that helps immensely. You pick an oracle card with an image of a dragonfly on it, and then later you walk to your car to see one on the door handle. These are all examples of the ways that the Spirit can communicate with you out in the real world. These sorts of messages always occur outside of you and require no effort from you other than your ability to go about your day as usual.

The clair spectrum, on the other hand, is an internal process and does require effort and acknowledgment from you—that is, your willingness to develop your Medial bridge and perceptual abilities. We can't force Spirit into sending us a sign or message, but we can work on becoming good listeners or receivers. Remember, we are in a partnership with Spirit, and like all partnerships, there should be a good level of respect and mutual give and take. So, next time you are in conversation, why not ask what you can do for Spirit or your higher self? Equally, learning to respect your own clair-abilities in relation to your everyday well-being and life is a must. After all, it is the very partnership that you have with yourself.

CHAPTER 12

THE SHADOW SIDE *OF* BEING MEDIAL

To be Medial is to be open. Open to communing with Spirit, open to speaking with Nature, open to picking up on energy from others. Open to listening to what your interior world is alerting you to, as well as to acknowledging the signs you see out in the world.

Openness is a wonderful tool that allows you to become a receptive channel, but most people are not taught how to properly control this inherent ability of being Medial. On top of this so many Medials, especially those who were born before the '90s, have had to contend with not only not understanding their own abilities but also not having many other Medials to turn to. This can be a very hard thing to experience as the true self tends to be hidden as a result, neatly tucked away and only shown to those deemed trustworthy enough. In response to this, the antidotal call then arrives to alert you to stand tall and to let others see you for who you really are—*a Medial*.

In the grand scheme, it is only relatively recently where all things Medial and mystically inclined have been so visibly celebrated. And as I mentioned earlier in this book the celebration of the Medial online is not the same thing as it being accepted on the ground, although it's a great start. For example, many medical mediums get ridiculed for their "outrageous" beliefs in clinics and hospitals, and yet they can have thousands of followers online or in a private practice. In essence, they often have to go at it alone if they want to both succeed and honor who they are. One can have a life online that is completely compartmentalized from their everyday lived experience, and so ideally the goal then is to be able to be oneself in all settings and environments.

Although the sad truth is that many places simply do not accept Medials. Many Medials have been left in the dark, stranded to the safety of the outskirts because they don't quite fit in. Either their ability to truly see makes those around them quite uncomfortable in their presence (a response which is either consciously or unconsciously evoked) or they simply do not feel and sense the world in the same way, and so this lends them to the propensity to feel safer and more at ease when they are alone.

For my modern-day Medials who are reading this, perhaps now then the unspoken complexity is learning how to maintain the sacred value of your Medial awareness without technology or other people using it for their advantage. You were born into a more connected time, largely due to technological advances, so it's important to have good boundaries with technology, which is often designed to keep you engaged all the time. These things are being woven as we speak, so adjustment and discernment are allies in our time. Ultimately, I can't tell you how to move with the times because the times are moving, but what I can say is that if you stay alert and awake, you will be able to pivot as required.

With this understanding, it is then helpful to know that being Medial is a gift, but at the same time it must be managed properly. So, no matter how society has viewed or currently views your Medial abilities, it is imperative to train your consciousness to open and close as needed, as well as set healthy boundaries all around. You do this for your own well-being, as well as for those around you. It is not healthy to be "open" all the time, nor is it healthy to have extremely rigid boundaries with people. Untrained Medials often distance themselves from other people (especially large groups) because it feels easier to do that than to experience the bombardment of psychic information that inadvertently comes through because they're too open.

In addition, it's not healthy to be hyper-connected, and as a result, many highly tech-orientated Medials feel very uncomfortable sitting alone without any distraction, especially if they have been using technology as a coping mechanism to avoid feeling what they are sensing and experiencing. The key here is understanding that this is all a balancing act that requires daily alertness. We all need connection, to be truly seen and understood by one another. We also need healthy boundaries: a good balance of being with people and having alone time. As well as maintaining healthy boundaries with technology, groupthink, and the depths of the collective unconscious. Medials must be able to be out in the world, functioning well, grounded in their lives, and I will share a few practices later that can begin to help with these things.

For now, let us acknowledge that it is often easy for Medials to drift into their inner worlds, as well as easily and quickly connect with the nonphysical sporadically throughout the day. And because of this, boundaries often feel fluid and even nonexistent at times. Yet, in our embodied 3D realities, boundaries are necessary for good health. **This leads us to the implicit kicker of being Medial: Because you are Medial, you can traverse boundaries that others may perceive as solid.** (For example, speaking to someone who has crossed over. Or even just daydreaming—just think about what and where you are viewing when you do this.) **But without healthy boundaries in your personal life, and with the unseen worlds, you can land up in the shadow space of being Medial. You need boundaries,** and at the same time, you know that with greater awareness that they don't really exist in concrete form.

This is the divine paradox of being Medial; because of it, it's essential to develop the skill set of being able to open and close your receptive channels as required. Or it is very likely that you will feel bombarded or even perhaps like your life isn't quite your own. You may get swept up in something that has absolutely nothing to do with you, even though you can clearly perceive it. In relation to this, I saw a social media post by a great podcaster that said, *Psychic or psychotic, there is no in-between.* And, oh, did I feel for her. Being too open will do exactly that.

If you are too open, it will feel like your radio station has tuned in to hundreds of different programs or frequencies all at the same time. Nothing will make sense, and information will flood the senses and obliterate the "receiver" in the process. It's like tuning in to a multitude of voices all clamoring at you at the same time. No wonder most Medials feel physically drained or even anxious when this happens. Being a healthy Medial means being absolutely grounded in this world, as well as being able to extend one's consciousness, when appropriate, to either the great beyond or one's own inner world. It is knowing when to zoom out and when to zoom in.

It is about daily self-care and community care in relation to how and when you choose to open up your Medial channel. Additionally, just because you may sense something about someone (even if it is something that would help them immensely), it does not mean it is *appropriate* to say what you are sensing. Finding the right timing is a healing quality in itself, and a well-balanced Medial knows both when to speak and when to keep quiet.

Toni Wolff maintained that a Medial Woman was a transmitter of the Spirit of her times. In her words, the "Medial woman is immersed in the psychic atmosphere of her environment and the Spirit of her period, but above all in the collective (impersonal) unconscious."[1] A good example of a Medial Woman of her time would be Joan of Arc. As history books tell us, Joan was a peasant girl who later became a heroine in France because she heard voices that instructed her as to what to do against the British army. The difficulty with Joan of Arc is that she was Medial to the detriment of everything else in her life—she became a martyr for the collective atmosphere of her time and, as a horrific result, was burned at the stake. (That said, I still imagine that she would have chosen the same path with or without more balanced boundaries because her calling was larger than her.) Ultimately, her time was not ready for a woman to wear men's clothes let alone have a peasant girl access divinity directly!

Yet in this book I have also shown how Medials do not just sense the impersonal collective unconscious but the personal one, too, especially when they learn how to use their abilities properly. For example, every time you get an intuitive "hit," as it relates to your own well-being, or simply work with a powerful dream, you are working with your personal unconscious. In my opinion, to be Medial is to be connected to both the personal and collective unconscious. That said, here is why all this matters: If you are open to receiving information about your environment, and the Spirit of your time, as well as your own stuff, you are dealing with huge swathes of information. And if you are too open, the information will be inundating. You may indeed oscillate between feeling psychic or unhinged. For Toni Wolff, this is where she expressed concern for the Medial Woman's shadow side. The shadow side appears when one lives a life that is too one-sided. In essence, if you are overfocused on your Medial abilities to the detriment of your life, family, friendships, love life, and work, then you are perhaps standing in the shadow realm of what it means to be Medial.

In relation to all of this, remember these four avenues that consistently need your attention:[2]

1. The aspect of nurturance in your life (toward self and others),
2. the way you support yourself (financial and otherwise),
3. relational intimacy (toward self and others),
4. and your Medial Nature.

To step out of the realm of shadow is to find the balance between these four quadrants and to adjust and maintain that balance as required. All four categories require your attention and focus in order for your well-being to flourish. This is a life's work, and the best way to really begin to heal any split between these quadrants is with a skilled expert. The reason being that because this is the basis for shadow work, it is often easier for someone outside of you to simply see what is obscured from your view. From my experience, working with someone can also save so much time and unnecessary heartache!

Toni Wolff then went on to further elaborate on the shadow aspects of being Medial, stating that when a Medial Woman lacks ego strength, she might be overcome by the effects of the unconscious.[3] She may also lack the capacity to discriminate between what comes from within herself and what comes from outside of her in relation to the collective unconscious. Healthy ego strength is developed by having a good grip on reality while also creating and maintaining healthy boundaries with everything nonphysical that you are sensing and perceiving. (A good way of thinking about the unconscious is that it is that which is unseen but still holds influence.) Everyday practices like clearing your energy, meditating, getting grounded, and having the good discipline to choose not to tap into everything that clamors for your attention will help immensely with this. Equally, understanding your own emotions and psychological triggers will help you to learn how to discern what is arising from within you, as opposed to what is being received from the unseen. In relation to this, here are a few good questions you can ask—first and foremost, **is this mine?**

Is this emotion mine? Is this thought mine? Is this place connected to something larger and am I just feeling the effects of it? Is "this" worth my attention?

If you are hitting up against situations that are echoes of your past, then you are likely dealing with internal structures that need changing. If, however, you are receiving or sensing information or feeling emotions that arise and disappear when you think about a particular situation or walk into a specific room, you may just simply be picking up on the energy of that place, person, or thing. This is where practice and discernment will come in. If you can learn to pay attention to what triggers a reaction in you throughout your day, you will come to see exactly what arises from within you, as opposed to what is outside of you. You will then come to feel your way around the edges of your own boundaries, as well as everything else you are interacting with.

Ask yourself these questions: *How did I wake up feeling? What shifted my mood so dramatically?* **Start to become less reactive and step into an observer role. Observe what arises and disappears. Pay no attention to what is immediate and learn to sit in the space that is neutral—drop into that sacred container that exists within you.** Remember, you can do this by simply getting still and silent. It can be as quick as a two-minute meditative and contemplative moment, which will help you to clearly experience your feelings, thoughts, and emotions and discern what they are alerting you to. If you can do this, you will create space between what you are feeling and how you feel called to respond in turn. Again, you are just receiving information; it does not need to feel all-consuming or even overwhelming, and the more frequently you practice this, the easier it usually gets.

Boundary work is imperative for Medials. This is something that may take a substantial amount of time to get right because Medials are often highly empathetic people. In regard to this, I highly recommend the book by Elaine Aron called *The Highly Sensitive Person: How to Thrive When the World Overwhelms You*. There is no other way to do this work than to become adept at looking within. Daily journaling about how you feel is a good place to start, as is staying on top of your own personal growth work, relationships, and the environments you interact with. Lack of boundaries feed the shadow side of a Medial and so creating and maintaining good boundaries creates a safe container for healthy expression, both for the Medial and those who interact with her. Again, it can be very helpful to work with an insightful therapist or coach who can help you unpack what is happening. We all have our blind spots, and Medials are no exception.

Let us now move on to the next marker that Toni Wolff presented in relation to the shadow side. A Medial might not be able to find the words to express the unconscious content she has access to. As a result, she might be confusing, and her influence on others and herself can even become destructive.[4]

Medials feel and pick up on so much, so it is important to be clear with those who you are communicating with, especially if you are giving them messages from the other side. People who feel disconnected from Spirit will often hold on to every word you say. They may also make decisions based off what you say, and as such, there are real-world consequences for any psychic and mediumistic information that you share. This is where ethics and training come in. In order to become any other form of licensed practitioner, ethics of practice are taught. Yet, with Medial abilities, this is not always the case, not because I think the vast majority of Medials want to do harm, but because they often find their own way in relation to understanding and developing their skill set. In this sense, it is up to each and every Medial to maintain a high standard of ethics if they offer any services, as well as anytime that they translate what they are perceiving to others. You are both receiving and sharing messages on behalf of Spirit, or from what you are seeing in the collective depths (can you discern the difference?), so if you are confused about what you are picking up on, it will impact you and those around you. Please don't give a message if it feels unclear or if it is distressing, and don't offer your services until you would be happy to receive them in kind. Help yourself and those around you by really developing your skill set.

Another hard thing Medials often come to discover is that because they can give a voice to what lies beneath the surface, it can make them uncomfortable to be around. Not everyone *wants* to see the shadows—or can stomach the truth, for that matter. So, learning when to tone it down or rein it in is also helpful—as is knowing when to shout it out from the rooftops! We all need relationships, and just as we need to feel safe with others, *people must equally feel safe with us.* Additionally, because Medials can sense what is happening beneath the surface, they may often feel upset or even outraged about the topside "showing and telling" done by the collective or a family system. In turn, other people may then find their anger or upset strange, disarming, off-putting, or "out of proportion" because they don't see it for themselves—or because they simply choose not to see the truth of the matter. In relation to this, I always think about the old story "The Emperor's New Clothes."

In essence, an emperor gets duped by two con men weavers who tell him that they are designing clothes that only the foolish and dumb cannot see. In fact, they don't weave any clothes but they go through the motions looming thin air. The court people then marvel at the magnificent nothingness being held up between the loom because they, too, do not want to look foolish or dumb for not "seeing" the beautiful clothes, when in fact there is absolutely nothing there! Eventually, the emperor parades down the street butt-naked with his invisible clothes, and all the town's people collude with the ridiculousness of the situation until a child blurts out, "The emperor is naked!"

A Medial would see the two con men (or family system) for what they are—*and a Wild Medial would stand in the town square and scream it out.* Or if the times were particularly violent, she may just slip away from the crowd and head back to the outskirts where foolishness often reigns less freely, leaving those in the town square to their own consequences, and by doing so she would kick in another mythic cycle, where she would then have to be coaxed back to society. And so, again we see that nothing is static and that movement is key, and so is creating your own community that understands you so that you don't have to drift alone toward the outskirts. You don't need to be a witch who lives out on the edges, although at times that thought is wildly tempting.

You also don't need to live in the shadow realm of being Medial—step out of the shadows by honoring all arenas of your life as valuable. Come out from hiding who you are. Declare it safe enough for you to be seen. Mediate on balance. Learn from teachers who have gone further than where you currently stand. Honor and love in your ability to discern what should be shared. Enjoy being embodied and allow yourself to be held in community. These are just a few things that can act as daily Soul balm, coaxing one out of the fear and confusion and into the realm of flourishment. In addition, please know that every person who resonates with these words is likely a person who you can connect with. Come and join us in our virtual circle. You can find more details on my site: athenalaz.com. And then, hopefully, one day in the not-so-distant future, perhaps society will change and Medials will become welcomed into all spaces.

THE SIMPLICITY OF WHAT IT MEANS TO OPEN UP AND CLOSE UP

As you've just read, one of the most difficult things for a Medial is often not learning how to be Medial but learning how to control their abilities. In fact, many of the Medials that I know are inherently psychic or tend toward mediumship. As a result, they often naturally gravitate to professions that can utilize their skill sets even if by proxy, like through healing, art, writing, teaching, research, and even police work. Often they simply weave healing and knowing no matter where they find themselves. Yet, as you've seen in the previous chapter, in the shadow realm of being, Medial boundaries are frequently either too rigid or too fluid, which can then create difficulties in other arenas of one's life, like sensing what another person is experiencing and telling them before they have a chance to figure it out for themselves. This can create havoc in an intimate relationship or in friendship circles, for example. For Medials, boundaries are intrinsically linked to one's ability to open and close their receptive channels at will. Of course, sometimes there will be messages that come through irrelevantly of how good you are at doing this. The goal is not perfection; it is to move toward greater well-being and personal understanding of what, when, and how you receive nonphysical or intuitive information. The first thing that you can do in this sense is to get really clear on what you have been doing up until this point. Take some time to journal answers to the following questions. There is no right way or wrong way of doing this—just be honest.

1. How do you receive insight and intuition?
2. How does it feel in your body?
3. Does it happen when you are in specific places?

4. When and where do you feel most relaxed and without external stimulation or receptive receiving?
5. When and where do you feel most open to your Medial abilities?
6. Do you immediately react to what you are sensing?
7. How do you respond to your intuitive hits? Do you write them down, speak about them, or dismiss them?
8. What do you do if you feel flooded or overwhelmed in large groups or simply by what you are sensing?
9. Do you eat junk food or drink lots of sugary drinks (or coffee) to numb your body out from what you are feeling and sensing?
10. Do you always seem to be "fixing" other people's problems?
11. Are you (or would you be) comfortable seeing Spirit?
12. Are you (or would you be) comfortable hearing Spirit?
13. Is it easier to "see" and "listen" internally, like in your mind's eye, for example?
14. Do you take the signs you see seriously, or do you secretly believe that they are just luck or coincidental?
15. Do the people around you know what you believe in?

If you take the time to answer these questions, you will get a baseline sense of how well you are handling your Medial abilities. You'll also see where you are when it comes to boundaries. Learning how to open and close your intuitive or receptive channels begins by first acknowledging that energy is real and that your body picks up on many aspects of the unseen without you needing to do actually consciously anything to "make this happen."

Now I want you to imagine the following scenario for about two minutes in your mind. Really focus on just *being* in the image as I describe it.

It is a beautiful hot summer's day and you find yourself in the perfect garden with a large and welcoming blue pool. See yourself floating in the water easily. There is no one around you, and you are free to be as you please. Stay in this imagery for as long as you like. If your thinking mind begins to introduce new aspects, simply focus on floating in the water. Bring your attention to the water and openness of the natural surroundings around you. Then, when you are ready, open your eyes and bring your attention back to the room.

How did that feel?

The goal of that mental imagery exercise was to show you how easily you can soften your body, relax your awareness, and become "open," like you are floating on water. When you work with the Medial Nature and your clair-senses, you will come to discover that energy means a great deal in how everything works together. You open your energy and tune in to specific focal points of awareness.

Now I want you to close your eyes and quickly imagine that you are standing somewhere and in the corner of your eye you sense someone running fast toward you. They're wearing a dark hoodie and you can't see their face. Open your eyes.

How did that make you feel? Did your chest contract? Did you hold your breath in response to the imagery? Did you close up?

These subtle changes are to show you how easy it is to open and close one's energy and that most of us naturally do this throughout the day without conscious thought that we are doing that very thing. We simply respond. The goal, then, is to become skilled at controlling your energy so that you are not hyperreactive to the environments you find yourself in. You innately actually know what "open" and "closed" feels like. You just did it in the two exercise above. It is simply learning to consciously direct your awareness while relaxing your body so that you can receive information without feeling overwhelmed. This takes practice.

In order to become highly proficient in managing your Medial abilities you must make a commitment to take this part of yourself seriously. You will need to carve out time and become consistent in your practice. Equally, I believe that many Medials will need to step out of their comfort zones and release old habits of defense or protection to move forward unencumbered by all that old "stuff." If you are really going to own who you are, you can't dance around the edges anymore; your boundaries will need to change. So, the best place to start is to ask yourself, *How do I treat this part of myself* and why? Take some time and journal your answer with utmost honesty. Then, when you get a chance, review what you've written so that you can understand the depths of what you are experiencing.

CHAPTER 13

THE MODERN MEDIATRIX *AND THE* CREATIVE PRINCIPLE REALIZED

In the shadow realm we are closed off and choked off from life. We fear a box that binds us without realizing that we can walk out at any time. Yet, when we walk toward unity, understanding, and self-acceptance, we discover that the box isn't concrete but ephemeral, made of shadows. We can turn our attention toward it and see it for what it truly is: a projection of the mind (personal or collective) or simply a tainted past playing on repeat. When you integrate the tools of wholeness that you discovered in the previous chapter, you move beyond the shadow realm of what it means to be Medial. And in doing so you free up stuck energy and move it toward more life-giving and redeeming experiences.

A Medial who is empowered gives voice to their abilities, the contents of the unconscious, and Spirit in a way that does not obliterate them or others. If they do this, they become what Toni Wolff called a Mediatrix. They understand the language of Spirit and psyche and works with both consciously. This is a huge task, and it is one often placed onto Medials from a young age. If you do not know your authentic voice, you will sit, muted, in the shallow of the shadows. If you don't honor the language of Spirit and psyche, you will feel overwhelmed by the depths of reality.

You must be honest with who you are and what you perceive. You must find both your own voice and give voice to the other side that you interact with. "Giving voice" can be through art, writing, talking, working with symbol and image, dancing, or any active psychic or Medial work. Move the image by giving it a voice. Move their stories by giving them a voice. Even in the depths of darkness, there is a way to move the image toward well-being. (Remember again that completion is in the act of doing, not in thinking about it.) When you do this, you free the image and transmute it into a new form—one orientated toward creative and life-giving principles.

This is what it means to be a Mediatrix. In creative living we are given an opportunity to resurrect our Souls, to breathe life into our lives, to move intrapsychic forces, and in doing so, we help make manifest that which we wish to see in the world. In creative living, we come to understand that it is the principle of grace that tends to both life and death. The very same grace that is activated every time you use your Medial Nature. Through this we discover that we hold the keys to consciousness, and in this space, we intimately learn that death is only distance and that Spirit is just one thought away.

CHAPTER 14

TOOLS *FOR* WHOLENESS

Before we dive into the tools for wholeness and well-being that I recommend, we need to look at a couple of foundational matters. First and foremost—authenticity matters, so please don't hide the truth of who you are! Hiding who you are creates tension within yourself and for those around you. It is like living a double life, which is both fracturing and tiring. One must find the courage to be true to oneself, and if this means being misunderstood or disliked by others, so be it. It is okay; your people will find you, especially once you begin to focus on meeting more like-minded people.

In relation to this many, Medials often receive information but dismiss it or simply choose not to act on it. This is an easy thing for many people to fall into (I have done this quite frequently over the course of my life). What I have found is that implicit beliefs are often what get in the way here, like, "You're strange or stupid for believing these things." Authentic living requires Medials to be true to themselves despite other people's judgment or any internalized critical judgment. This is basic self-love work and is at the root of authentic living. If this is something you struggle with, I recommend the books *You Can Heal Your Life* and *Mirror Work* by Louise Hay.[1]

Another foundational issue that many Medials press up against is that the information they are receiving may not be real. The easiest way to knock that belief out is simply to start acting on the intuitive impulses you receive. Treat it like a fun game and it will become one! This is also a very helpful way to start proving to yourself that the information you receive is not only true but also accurate. Test this information out for yourself first. For example, you could say, "I would like to receive information on what color T-shirt the next person who I see will be." (When I first started out, I preferred testing things that didn't require me to speak to anyone, as I didn't want to share information that could unintentionally hurt another person.)

Additionally, when Spirit or the nonphysical part of you (the Soul) communicates with you, they/it can often place an additional sense of responsibility onto us. Here we often discover that as we work with our intuitive abilities more frequently, the information we receive often becomes less about us and more about other people. So make no mistake, Spirit may work with you to heal the collective.

In this sense, I think of an experience that an author shared at the International Association for the Study of Dreams. In a dream, this person was told to reach out to a friend whom he hadn't spoken to in over a decade and give him $10,000. On waking, he didn't do anything about the dream. Fast-forward some time, and a dream or two later with the same message, he knew what he had to do. He spoke to his wife, and they agreed about the money. He then called his friend and told him what happened. It turned out his friend wasn't in a good way and that he really needed the money to help his dad, who was very ill.

Here we see that it is not always easy to act on intuitive information on first impulse—especially when the information asks you to be of great service. I once again think of Joan of Arc here and of all the other Medials out there in the daily trenches who quietly make the lives of those around them better. Many hospice workers fall into this category because they are often the ones who validate the many Spirit/nonphysical experiences that dying people experience on the threshold of death, such as deathbed visions or speaking to their deceased loved ones because they are in the room with them. If you are interested in reading more of these types of shared death experiences, I refer you to the work of the Shared Crossing Project by William Peters (M.A., M.Ed., M.F.T.).[2] There are so many ways to be of service, and we are all called in our own ways, and often it comes down to just being very honest about what we experience. Let us now dive in to some tools that can help Medials reach greater well-being and wholeness.

Tool 1: Remove any self-enforced barriers or beliefs that get in the way

Anyone who has ever struggled to fall asleep and remain asleep will know that most of the information centered around "fixing" this issue is actually about removing the conditioned barriers to good sleep. Of course, this only applies if someone doesn't have an underlying physical issue that is impacting their sleep. For our purposes, I'm talking about the general nonsleepers who can't seem to remember how to fall asleep. People will often offer guidance like sleep in a dark room, no bright lights, no technology before bed, use comfortable sheets, etc. In essence, these things help prime one for sleep, and they also help to minimize sensory distraction, but in the grand scheme, they don't actually tell you how to fall asleep. Sleeping is a natural response, one that we all have been doing since we were born.

Everyone knows how to sleep, but so many people do not allow themselves to do so because they've conditioned themselves to worry the minute they get into bed. Sleep isn't the issue; the mind is. In the same way, being Medial means removing any self-enforced barriers and beliefs that get in the way. **Get the thinking around what it means to be Medial clear, and being Medial then becomes clear.** Your thoughts and beliefs can and will influence your ability to connect to Spirit and the depths of your own unconscious, as well as that of the collective. You must believe that it is easy to connect, and then it becomes easy as a result. Here are a few common beliefs and actions that can get in the way of receiving intuitive information:

BELIEF: ONLY "GIFTED" PEOPLE ARE INTUITIVE.

After working with many people who did not think they were intuitive until they began to practice, I can say with confidence that being gifted often has nothing to do with it. Removing social conditioning and practicing does more for the skill set than innate talent. You are worthy and have always been of receiving intuitive information, and if you do not feel this way, then please work with someone who can help you develop positive self-esteem in this regard. You can also join my community where you can interact with like-minded people.

BELIEF: IT'S HARD TO CONNECT.

This may be true at the beginning, but with time and consistency, this changes. Often it is hard to connect because the ability has been shut down so much that one needs to really consciously awaken it. You do this by remaining disciplined. Keep practicing, and only stop when you start seeing results.

BELIEF: I DON'T HAVE THE TIME.

Many people often tell me that they don't feel like they have enough time. I can empathize with this. The question is, can you afford to *not* map out the time? Even five minutes in the shower to get your energy clear and zipped up (see tool 4) will help you begin to change your relationship to your intuition. Many people also have an image of receiving intuitive insights as something you can only do after sitting for hours on a meditation mat (this is true), but, really, as you've seen over the course of this book, intuition can come through at any time if you are open to receiving it. Just think about your clair-senses and moving through your day. You naturally pick up on information, but you may simply not be paying enough attention to what you are perceiving because you are not present. In other words, bring your attention to the here and now as often as you can, and you will start to experience your intuition more often.

You can stop the thinking mind by focusing your awareness and bringing your attention to your surroundings and how you feel in your body. List four things you can see and three things that you can touch. List two things that you can hear. List one thing you can taste. By doing these simple mindfulness practices, you begin to take ownership of where your attention is focused. The more frequently that you do this, the easier it becomes to soften the focus on the flood of your thoughts. Your thoughts will still continue, but they will take a back seat to where you are placing your attention. By doing this, you are retraining your awareness so that you may be able to step into an observer role more frequently. It takes practice and commitment to hold steady to a meditative practice. There is work to be done here, and it is so easy to simply want to tap out. We're all human, but this is one of the categories that must change if you want to really begin to take your Medial abilities seriously.

Tool 2: Unplug from mainstream consciousness

In our current reality, distraction is everywhere. Technology can be incredibly helpful, but it is also a tool that can become addictive. As such, we must be honest with ourselves as to how much time we are spending scrolling for the sake of simply being so used to doing just that. If you can, put a screen timer on your phone and see how much time you spend watching and consuming information. We are free to choose what we want to participate in, and this is entirely up to you. However, if you want to really develop your Medial abilities, you must acknowledge that a lot of the noise from mainstream consciousness is of a harsh consciousness. Violence, conflict, division, and hate flood our screens, and we often can't help but react (even if you don't actually respond online) to what we are perceiving. In order to receive higher-order information, one must first unplug from mainstream consciousness.

Your awareness is the greatest asset you have. It is what helps you to co-create in this world. It is the tool that helps you to experience life in all its complexity, and it is what lets you experience what goes beyond this physical realm. Please don't farm it out for the sake of mindless distraction.

Tool 3: Your body is as important as your psychic abilities

Many Medials who have not yet learned how to intentionally open and close their Medial abilities will often drink a lot of coffee and eat sugary foods to try to numb out the sensory overload that they experience. This is not a healthy long-term strategy, even though it may work momentarily. It is a psychological short-term-relief strategy that doesn't address the underlying issue, which is often the fear of being flooded, overwhelmed, or engulfed by what you are sensing—in other words, the fear of being "swallowed up" by what one is sensing and feeling, so one turns to food and swallows it up as a compensatory measure.

The antidote is to ground and center, to remember that you can open and close up as required. You simply do this by first addressing how you feel: "I am overwhelmed." Then take your shoes off (if you are in a space where you can) and bring your full attention to your feet. How do they feel? What is the texture beneath the soles of your feet? Just focus on your feet. Then picture your feet "growing" roots that go all the way down through the floor into the earth. If you can, then also bring your attention to your breathing. Release any tension in your face, jaw, and body. Relax your shoulders and consciously breathe in and out in a way that feels soothing and not forced. This can take two minutes to do and often helps make one feel both grounded and centered. This is a mindfulness practice that works, and it is yours for the taking.

It may also be helpful to later jot down the trigger related to the information that made you feel overwhelmed and engulfed, as it may be something you need to personally work on or simply a comfort zone that you may need to step out of. If you have awareness of "the trigger" you can get beyond it without becoming reactive. In addition, many Medials find it very hard to be embodied. They find it easier to be traversing the ether than to be grounded in the density of what everything physically feels like. So, practices like walking every day and eating well can really help with this. Your body is important, and in order to be balanced, you must acknowledge its needs and health. This is a daily and lifelong nonnegotiable practice.

Tool 4: Energetic boundaries

Here's my rule: Zip it up and open up.
Close it up and ground.
You "zip up your energy" first thing in the morning and when you are alone. You can do this in the bathroom if need be. First, mentally clear your energy of anything negative or stagnant. If you are standing in the shower, you can also imagine the water flowing and cleansing your energy while picturing anything heavy or mucky simply going down the drain. Then, when you are out of the shower, picture yourself zipping up your energy, just as if you are stepping into a protective bubble that zips up around you. The bubble is about an elbow's length away from your body, and nothing energetic can enter this space without your permission.

Equally, you can do this practice before you start any intuitive session or meditative practice. The goal is to consciously work with your energy. In meditation, you know that you are opening up your consciousness to perceive alternative realities or nonphysical information. This is easiest when you feel relaxed and at ease. These energetic practices help with these things. Then, once you have received psychic/mediumistic insight or simply have been contemplative for long enough, it is necessary to close your psychic channels so that you don't get overwhelmed moving about the rest of your day. You can verbally say, "I am now closing my receptive channels from all nonphysical information unless it is imperative for me to know for the highest good." You can also bring your energy back to you by imagining your "energy" (however you see it) as coming back toward you. Then practice grounding again (see tool 3) and practice focusing on your feet.

Tool 5: Delineating dual awareness

One of the most common errors I hear from people practicing is that they think that their thinking minds must be absolutely quiet in order to receive insights. Of course, the less clutter of thoughts, the better, but it is actually quite normal for thoughts to arise in conjunction with intuitive insights. As such, it is necessary to delineate dual awareness. You know what a barrage of thinking is; it goes on and on like a train. It is often tangential and moves from one concept or thing to the next. That is the thinking mind's job—to think—so it is often easier not to fight it but to simply learn to witness it.

Intuitive insights, on the other hand, are very clear. They have weight and carry a certain resonance to them. In essence, they feel like they land or "drop in." So, the more you simply step into the observer role, you will be able to delineate this type of dual awareness. I have found that I often receive psychic information on what feels like the right-hand side of my awareness. When I practice conscious focus in my dreamwork, it feels like it arises front and center, about a meter away from my eyes. These are personal cues that I have picked up over time. If you practice, you will begin to discover your own. And remember, some people don't experience their intuition in this way ever—it's all about learning what personally works for you. Trial and error is the name of the game at the beginning of learning how to work with nonphysical information.

Tool 6: Observe, don't absorb

Every time you walk into a place and start to pick up on cues around you, remind yourself that you can observe without absorbing. If someone's energy feels too intense, simply ground (a five-second focus on your feet) and then push your energetic bubble out. It's like returning a letter back to a sender in real time.

In meditation or in your intuitive sessions with other people, again observe, and don't absorb. If by the end of the session you feel overwhelmed, fatigued, or tired, then clear your energy and practice self-care.

I once watched a medium who told the audience that he felt like his chest was closing, and he knew in that moment that the deceased coming through had died from some type of issue related to the chest. It turned out that the person had indeed died in an accident and that his lungs had been crushed as a result. This may seem like a very intense experience for a medium to go through, and it can be if they don't know what is happening. But mainly, the relay of information is being received through the energy "body," so it doesn't feel as intense as it sounds and is often fleeting. The feeling also doesn't remain once the message has been shared, and most mediums know how to work with this flow of energy and information once they have received some training on the matter.

Remember, you are simply there to observe. You do not need to absorb the experience as happening to you. It's like participating in an interactive show. You watch and feel for a while and then return to your life totally unencumbered.

Tool 7: Witness and receive information without judgment or labeling

It is natural to form opinions and label things, as this is how we makes sense of the world. We see a dog, and then we label it a dog in a split second, after which we often place our judgment onto it: "What a cute little Chihuahua" or "What a yappy dog." The art of being Medial is simply listening to what you are receiving without trying to "make sense" of everything. This isn't to say that you can't ask for clarity with the guides or nonphysical part of yourself that you are interacting with. It is just to say that it is often easier (and wiser!) to listen without placing judgments or labels onto what you are receiving in the exact moment of receiving it. I once got a clairaudient message to visit a family member. "Go next Saturday," the voice said. That was it, the whole message. It turned out that next Saturday they had a heart attack.

Tool 8: Don't share with those set on never understanding you

No matter the evidence presented, some people will simply refuse to see beyond the physical. In this case, it is easier and often less painful to simply not share with those absolutely bent on not understanding your point of view.

Tool 9: Don't make decisions for other adults

Medials often struggle with this because they can perceive helpful information. That said, it is not—I repeat, it is not—your responsibility to clean someone else's side of the street. The other adults must make their own decisions and live with the associated consequences as a result. It is human nature that when we feel alone, lost, or afraid, to want to hand our decision-making abilities over to other people, but Medials need to be particularly wary of picking up these kinds of requests. Of course, you can share in a way that feels good to you, but having awareness of this dynamic is helpful and healthy so that you don't unintentionally become responsible for other people's decisions.

Tool 10: Kind heart, kind words

I have yet to receive a message from Spirit that did not help in some shape or form. I know that it is not my genius ego thinking up these things. Information flows from the nonphysical through to me and I then receive and share it. Spirit or your own higher consciousness is doing the work of sending you information, and you are doing the work of receiving it—that is, of being a clear channel so that you don't muddle up the message. It takes two here, and it is helpful to remain humble in this process. It is also helpful to extend the kindness you receive from Spirit out toward others. Now, this isn't to say that if you get insight about someone's health, you shouldn't share the message with them because they might find it distressing. It is, however, to say that there is an empathetic, appropriate, and ethical way of sharing all received information.

Tool 11: Let others love and take care of you

You don't need to be needed to be loved. If you never shared anything helpful in a Medial sense with anyone, that would also be okay. If that feels like a hard pill to swallow, then I recommend the book *Codependent No More* by Melody Beattie.

Tool 12: If people abandon you, don't abandon yourself in response

Medials walk to the beat of a different drum, and sometimes this just doesn't work for other people. So, if you have been abandoned and rejected for being too (enter whatever label here), please don't abandon yourself in return. You are needed here and are as valuable as any other strand in this cosmic web that we call life.

Tool 13: Who are you without your medial abilities?

Again, this is a reminder to develop other avenues of your life and skill set. After all, we are in this realm even though we can perceive others, so it is up to us to enjoy (and actually) live out our embodied experience with presence. This is the category of shadow work that we discussed in the previous chapter. If you are overidentified with being a Medial, it may be time to bring more balance and joy back into your life by expanding your life to include a diverging range of interests and relationships.

Tool 14: Intentional alone time and social time

Wild Medials need more time alone than those who don't identify as such. You must map out time to be able to stop the noise and bombardment from the external world. You do not need to do anything constructive in this intentional time of solitude. Being in nature, lying on the ground, and feeling the wind on your face is enough. As is lying in a room with the curtains drawn and just resting. A hot bath can work wonders too. On the flip side, for those Medials who also struggle with being social because it is too overwhelming, you must try to help yourself in this arena. Social well-being is the counterbalance for being alone. Start small and then work your way toward having a healthy and active (for you in whatever way you deem fit) social life. A good book club can be a healthy and easy start. Remember, all this is about balance and not perfection.

Remember, you do not need to be "on" all day long. If you choose to go into a profession that requires your Medial skill set, then you will need to work this out for yourself. Ultimately, you can map out boundaries with your own thinking, your Medial abilities, Spirit, and other people. Be good to you. Be good to others.

Tool 15: Joy and love are high vibrational frequencies

It can be easy to fall into seriousness and pervasive doing. But so often the message from Spirit is simple: Find joy in the now and love others and yourself. It's not meant to be all doom and gloom. We are meant for joy too. So, if you are swimming in the depths of collective and/or personal pain, remind yourself to come up for air.

CHAPTER 15

THE WILDFLOWERS OF YOUR HEART

Our time together has almost come to an end, but before that happens, I would like to dip into one more story—a narrative that I originally heard on the *Living Myth* podcast, hosted by Michael Meade.[1] This is a true story about a physicist and philosopher named Gustav Fechner who lived in the 1800s and whose words you are about to read:

"Man lives upon the earth not once, but three times. The first stage of life is a continuous sleep; the second is an alternation between sleeping and waking; the third is an eternal waking. In the first stage man lives alone in darkness; in the second he lives with companions, near and among others, but detached and in a light which pictures for him the exterior; in the third his life is merged with that of other Souls into the higher life of the Supreme, and he discerns the reality of ultimate things."[2]

As you have seen over the course of this book, to be a Medial is to be one with the mystery of the liminal, to hover in the threshold between what was and what will be. And yet, through Fechner's words, we also see that we are often in the in-between as humans. We stand in the center of the second stage—an alteration between waking and sleeping—and between the unseen and seen worlds mediating the two with our very own awareness. We know that we are of this world and yet not of it at the very same time. And as you've come to see over the course of this book, to be Medial is to switch on our inner sight so that we can see through any time period or experience through the eyes of our Souls.

Fechner experienced what many people would consider extreme darkness. In what seemed to be a harsh stroke of fate, he went blind while doing experiments that involved human sight. As a man of science who had spent a large portion of his life working, his Spiritual awakening hit hard. As a result, he had to remain in a darkened room in his house, where he often found himself alone and in silence. He was in many ways forced within. Collectively, we, too, know what that experience has felt like, albeit in a different way. His dark night of the Soul lasted many years where he quite literally sat alone in the darkness. I tried to imagine what that experience must have felt like for him, and the word that came up for me was *harrowing*.

Fechner sat in that dark room *for years* as his physical and mental health began to severely deteriorate. He even found himself unable to digest food after a failed medical experience, and as a result, he began to face starvation. During that time he couldn't work, and he had no helpful distractions. Eventually he wasn't even able to listen to others reading stories to him. He was in a form of his own self-described oblivion. I imagine what he must have endured in that daily darkness while being unable to digest quite literally and metaphorically what was happening to him. And yet, unbeknown to him, while his old identity was dying a slow and painful death, a truer form was being woven in the limen. As he sat and endured that dark room, his Soul sight was returning to him ever so slightly and slowly.

In parallel we see that even during our own times of darkness, when we feel like we are suffering and that things seem hopeless, that is when we must remember that quietly in the ether new life is being woven. We must remember that dark times do not last forever. Even wars do not last—to date, they have always ended. And if a war is raging within you, then this also applies: No darkness can endure a greater awareness that arises from within. Lucidity of awareness illuminates a new reality—especially when we begin to think together in this way. In any times of darkness, either personal or collective, we can soften into surrender and rely on a strength far greater than that of physicality. We can rely on the strength of our Spirits and the support of those who love us. For Fechner it was the love of his wife and his Spiritual faith that kept him going. Love and faith are the two cures for fear and darkness and the two things we freely have access to.

It is equally helpful to remember that when we are engulfed from the outside, our inner space naturally expands as a counterbalance. And in this space, we discover that wisdom and knowledge have always held hands and that right and wrong are siblings who often help us discover our own energetic creations. In the limen, we discover that our deep-hearted self who lives in the waking world can just as easily exist in the potent realms of the darkness. In this roomy space, we discover that *we are* what traverses both realms, and we choose to go to each as necessary—whether consciously or unconsciously.

In the end we remember that we already are the Strong Sighted Self, who can see in all realms.

Sometimes sitting in the dark is the only way to become a beginner again. Sometimes it is the only way to remember. We can willingly choose to sit in the darkness and allow the silence to engulf us so that we can understand ourselves more clearly. Then, through what feels like no movement, a new pathway is forged, and things outside in the material world move of their own accord.

We discover that we can shed many skins in just this one life. Most Medials do.

Often, we also do this shedding in the potent depths of what Fechner described as an oblivion. And as author Michael Meade revealed in response to this, "When you come to the end of what you know, you can stand at the edge of the light or you can step into the darkness, and then two things can either happen. You can fly or you can plummet into an endless emptiness."[3]

How refreshingly truthful.

Yet, if you leap, you will discover that we are made for both the depths and the distance. One can both fly and free-fall—*and neither are to be feared.*

In the great depths of the unknown, Fechner found the endless emptiness and came out of the experience with numinous sight. His release from darkness came in the form of his neighbor—a woman who dreamed of a food that would cure his ailment. How "lucky" that he lived next door to a Medial Woman—or was it simply once again the hand of fate? It seems that in the threshold of our lives, we can choose to greet fate and destiny as two old friends who show up right on time, just as Fechner's neighbor did.

In response, Fechner began to eat, and his health started to restore itself. On his own accordance, he said that his eyes began to feel a real "hunger for the light," and as a result he began to exercise them. And just like that, on a random day in October, he walked outside and was able to see again. He opened his eyes and he saw an ensouled life—that is, the Soul woven through all life. He saw the true essence of every living thing. And as a result of his experiences, Fechner wrote a book about the Soul of plants and trees, and it became a bestseller for over 74 years. In his own words:

The whole garden seemed to me transformed, as if not I but all of nature were arisen anew; and I thought, it is only a matter of opening my eyes again to allow a nature grown old to become young again.[4]

Fechner discovered that there was no separation between him and what he was seeing, which was the living, breathing pulse of the world around him. For the first time in a very long time, he saw separation for the illusion that it is. He saw this because he had been forced to look within and then anew. With clear sight he then opened his mind, and in that moment:

He saw the Soul of life in the shape of trees and leaves and the gentle fern seed.
He saw a Wild Medial life.
And now it's time for you to do the same thing.
To close the door to this book,
to step out and see
with the wildflowers of your heart.

ACKNOWLEDGMENTS

My deepest gratitude to Reid Tracy, Patricia Gift, and Anna Cooperberg for welcoming me into the Hay House family with such incredible warmth, support, and generosity. To Louise Hay in Spirit, I am so grateful for you and your words that once helped me heal. Thank you, Coleen O'Shea, for your guidance and expertise. To my husband, Jed, thank you for the beautiful life that we share together. To our families, we love you. And most importantly, to you, reading this—thank you for journeying with me!

ABOUT THE AUTHOR

Athena Laz is a Medial Woman, counseling psychologist, and intuitive. She lives on the East Coast and offers an array of programs and workshops which can be viewed on her website. She is also the best-selling author of *Sisterhood of the Seers Oracle Deck*, *The Alchemy of Your Dreams: A Modern Guide to Lucid Dreaming and Interpretation*, and *The Deliberate Dreamer's Journal*. Her work has been translated into 13 languages worldwide and has been featured in many media outlets such as the *Today* show, *Publishers Weekly*, and the Shift Network. You can find more information about her work at **www.athenalaz.com**.

ENDNOTES

INTRODUCTION: THE RETURN OF THE SOUL VOICE
1. James Hillman, *Re-Visioning Psychology* (New York: William Morrow, 1997).

CHAPTER 1: WE BEGIN WITH A MEDIAL WOLFF
1. Toni Wolff, *Structural Forms of the Feminine Psyche*, trans. Paul Watzlawik (Zurich, 1956), 4.
2. Wolff, *Structural Forms of the Feminine Psyche*, 4.

CHAPTER 2: THE THRESHOLD OF ENTRY
1. Joseph Campbell, *Mythic Worlds, Modern Words: On the Art of James Joyce*, ed. Edmund L. Epstein, Ph.D. (Novato, California: New World Library, 1993).

CHAPTER 3: MEDIATRIX OF ALL GRACES
1. "I Am Your Mother," Dominican Friars Foundation, 2024, https://dominicanfriars.org/mother.
2. "Basilica of Guadalupe," *Encyclopaedia Britannica*, https://www.britannica.com/topic/Basilica-of-Guadalup.
3. "Where Do We Go From Here?," Stanford University, The Martin Luther King, Jr., Research and Education Institute, https://kinginstitute.stanford.edu/where-do-we-go-here.

CHAPTER 4: THE MEDIAL WOMAN'S MYTHIC JOURNEY OF INITIATION
1. Clarissa Pinkola Estés, Ph.D., *Women Who Run with the Wolves: Myths and Stories of the Wild Woman Archetype* (New York: Ballantine, 1992), 23.
2. Estés, *Women Who Run with the Wolves*, 22.
3. Jeremiah Curtin, "Go to the Verge of Destruction and Bring Back Shmat-Razum," *Myths and Folk-Tales of the Russians, Western Slavs, and Magyars* (Boston: Little, Brown, and Company, 1890), 179.

CHAPTER 5: AN ANCIENT LANGUAGE IS EVOKED
1. Jeremiah Curtin, "Go to the Verge of Destruction and Bring Back Shmat-Razum," *Myths and Folk-Tales of the Russians, Western Slavs, and Magyars* (Boston: Little, Brown, and Company, 1890), 264.

CHAPTER 6: THE BABA YAGA EFFECT

1. Jeremiah Curtin, "Go to the Verge of Destruction and Bring Back Shmat-Razum," *Myths and Folk-Tales of the Russians, Western Slavs, and Magyars* (Boston: Little, Brown, and Company, 1890).
2. Clarissa Pinkola Estés, Ph.D., *Women Who Run with the Wolves: Myths and Stories of the Wild Woman Archetype* (New York: Ballantine, 1992), 25.
3. Estés, *Women Who Run with the Wolves*, 22.
4. Craig Foster and Swati Thiyagarajan, dirs., *The Animal Communicator*, 2012; The Roku Channel.
5. Estés, *Women Who Run with the Wolves*, 325.
6. Curtin, "Go to the Verge of Destruction."
7. Curtin, "Go to the Verge of Destruction."

CHAPTER 7: ROLL THAT MEDIAL BALL UNTIL YOU LAND IN THE WILD WOODS

1. Jeremiah Curtin, "Go to the Verge of Destruction and Bring Back Shmat-Razum," *Myths and Folk-Tales of the Russians, Western Slavs, and Magyars* (Boston: Little, Brown, and Company, 1890).
2. TED, "Your elusive creative genius | Elizabeth Gilbert," posted February 9, 2009, YouTube, https://youtu.be/86x-u-tz0MA.

CHAPTER 8: WHEN ALL HOPE IS LOST AND RETURNING HOME

1. Jeremiah Curtin, "Go to the Verge of Destruction and Bring Back Shmat-Razum," *Myths and Folk-Tales of the Russians, Western Slavs, and Magyars* (Boston: Little, Brown, and Company, 1890), 179.
2. Curtin, "Go to the Verge of Destruction," 179.

CHAPTER 9: IN THE SILENCE, THE ORACLE SPEAKS

1. "Dodona. The Oracle of Sounds. Oracular Tablets," Acropolis Museum, 2018, https://www.theacropolismuseum.gr/en/multimedia/dodona-oracle-sounds-oracular-tablets.
2. Dave Chaffey, "Global Social Media Statistics Research Summary May 2024," Smart Insights, May 1, 2024, https://www.smartinsights.com/social-media-marketing/social-media-strategy/new-global-social-media-research.
3. Ashley Strickland, "Mysterious Species Buried Their Dead and Carved Symbols 100,000 Years Before Humans," CNN, June 7, 2023, https://www.cnn.com/2023/06/05/world/homo-naledi-burials-carvings-scn.
4. "Rising Star," National Geographic Society, https://www.nationalgeographic.org/society/our-programs/rising-star.
5. Mark Mannucci, dir., *Unknown Cave of Bones*, 2023; Netflix.
6. Martin Shaw, *Red Bead Woman: Consequence and Longing in the Myth World* (Devon, England: Cista Mystica Press, 2020).

7. Daniel Gorman Jr., "Revisiting Joseph Campbell's The Power of Myth," *Intermountain West Journal of Religious Studies* 5, no. 1 (2014), https://digitalcommons.usu.edu/imwjournal/vol5/ iss1/5.

CHAPTER 10: LEARNING TO SEE AND HEAR IN A SACRED MANNER

1. Happiness & Its Causes, "JOURNEY INTO DREAMTIME with Aunty Munya Andrews at HAP22," posted November 15, 2022, YouTube, https://youtu.be/n5XUxyNGLTg.
2. Nicola Wilson Clasby, "Disarming the Shout of Doom: Chopra's Alkahest," *UNIversitas: Journal of Research, Scholarship, and Creative Activity* 4, no. 1 (2008): Article 5, https://scholarworks.uni.edu/universitas/vol4/iss1/5.

CHAPTER 11: UNDERSTANDING YOUR OWN INTUITIVE ABILITIES

1. Rupert Sheldrake, *The Sense of Being Stared At: And Other Unexplained Powers of the Human Mind* (Rochester, Vermont: Inner Traditions/Bear, 2013).
2. Anita Moorjani, *Dying to Be Me: My Journey from Cancer, to Near Death, to True Healing* (Carlsbad, CA: Hay House, 2022).

CHAPTER 12: THE SHADOW SIDE OF BEING MEDIAL

1. Toni Wolff, *Structural Forms of the Feminine Psyche*, trans. Paul Watzlawik (Zurich, 1956).
2. Wolff, *Structural Forms of the Feminine Psyche*.
3. Wolff, *Structural Forms of the Feminine Psyche*.
4. Wolff, *Structural Forms of the Feminine Psyche*.

CHAPTER 14: TOOLS FOR WHOLENESS

1. Louise Hay, *You Can Heal Your Life* (Carlsbad, CA: Hay House, 1984); and *Mirror Work* (Carlsbad, CA: Hay House, 2016).
2. William Peters (M.A., M.Ed., MFT). The Shared Crossing Project, https://www.sharedcrossing.com.

CHAPTER 15: THE WILDFLOWERS OF YOUR HEART

1. Michael Meade, "What the Soul Sees," *Living Myth* podcast, episode 349, Mosaic Multicultural Foundation, 2024, https://www.mosaicvoices.org/episode-349-what-the-soul-sees.
2. Gustav Theodor Fechner, *The Little Book of Life After Death* (Newburyport, MA: Weiser Books, 2005).
3. Meade, "What the Soul Sees."
4. Frederick C. Beiser, "Gustav Theodor Fechner," Stanford University, Center for the Study of Language and Information, January 12, 2020, https://plato.stanford.edu/archIves/sum2020/entries/fechner.

Hay House Titles of Related Interest

YOU CAN HEAL YOUR LIFE, the movie,
starring Louise Hay & Friends
(available as an online streaming video)
www.hayhouse.co.uk/louise-movie

THE SHIFT, the movie,
starring Dr. Wayne W. Dyer
(available as an online streaming video)
Learn more at www.hayhouse.co.uk/the-shift-movie

ARCHETYPES: Who Are You?
by Caroline Myss

*RISE SISTER RISE: A Guide to Unleashing the Wise,
Wild Woman Within* by Rebecca Campbell

*THE PROPHETESS: The Return of the Prophet from
the Voice of the Divine Feminine* by Chelan Harkin

*THE FAIRY TALE HEROINE ORACLE A 48-Card
Deck and Guidebook* by Sharon Blackie

All of the above are available at your local bookstore,
or may be ordered by contacting Hay House (see next page).

We hope you enjoyed this Hay House book. If you'd like to receive our online catalogue featuring additional information on Hay House books and products, please contact:

Hay House UK Ltd
1st Floor, Crawford Corner,
91–93 Baker Street, London W1U 6QQ
Tel: +44 (0)20 3927 7290; www.hayhouse.co.uk

Published in the United States of America by:
Hay House LLC
PO Box 5100, Carlsbad, CA 92018-5100
Tel: (760) 431-7695 or (800) 654-5126
www.hayhouse.com

Published in Australia by:
Hay House Australia Publishing Pty Ltd
18/36 Ralph St., Alexandria NSW 2015
Tel: +61 (02) 9669 4299
www.hayhouse.com.au

Published in India by:
Hay House Publishers (India) Pvt Ltd
Muskaan Complex, Plot No. 3,
B-2, Vasant Kunj, New Delhi 110 070
Tel: +91 11 41761620
www.hayhouse.co.in

Let Your Soul Grow

Experience life-changing transformation – one video at a time – with guidance from the world's leading experts.

www.healyourlifeplus.com

TRANSFORM YOUR DAY— ANYTIME, ANYWHERE

With the **Empower You** Unlimited Audio *App*

66 ⭐⭐⭐⭐⭐ **Life changing.**
My fav app on my entire phone, hands down! – Gigi **99**

Unlimited access to the entire Hay House audio library!

You'll get:

- 600+ soul-stirring **audiobooks** to expand your mind
- 1,000+ **meditations** for restful sleep, morning focus, and gentle healing
- Bite-sized audios **under 20 minutes**—perfect for busy days
- **Exclusive talks** you won't find anywhere else
- **Daily affirmations**
- Fresh content added **every week** to fuel your journey

New audios added every week!

66 Driving, yard work, and housework have been **transformed**! – Ruffles27 **99**

Scan the QR code to start listening or visit **hayhouse.com/unlimited**

CONNECT WITH
HAY HOUSE
ONLINE

 hayhouse.co.uk    @hayhouse

 @hayhouseuk    @hayhouseuk.bsky.social

 @hayhouseuk    @HayHousePresents

Find out all about our latest books & card decks • Be the first to know about exclusive discounts • Interact with our authors in live broadcasts • Celebrate the cycle of the seasons with us • Watch free videos from your favourite authors • Connect with like-minded souls

'The gateways to wisdom and knowledge are always open.'

Louise Hay